RAISING KIDS ...
without breaking the bank

THE PARENT'S GUIDE TO MONEY

Stella Tarakson

ALLEN&UNWIN

First published in 2004

83 Alexander Street
Crows Nest NSW 2065
Australia
Phone: (61 2) 8425 0100
Fax: (61 2) 9906 2218
E-mail: info@allenandunwin.com
Web: www.allenandunwin.com

National Library of Australia
Cataloguing-in-Publication entry:

Tarakson, Stella.
Raising kids . . . without breaking the bank: the parent's guide to money.

Includes index.
ISBN 1 74114 190 7.

1. Parents—Finance, Personal. 2. Child rearing.
I. Title.

332.024

Set in 11/13 pt Meridien Roman by Midland Typesetters, Maryborough, Victoria
Printed by Southwood Press Pty Limited, Sydney

10 9 8 7 6 5 4 3 2 1

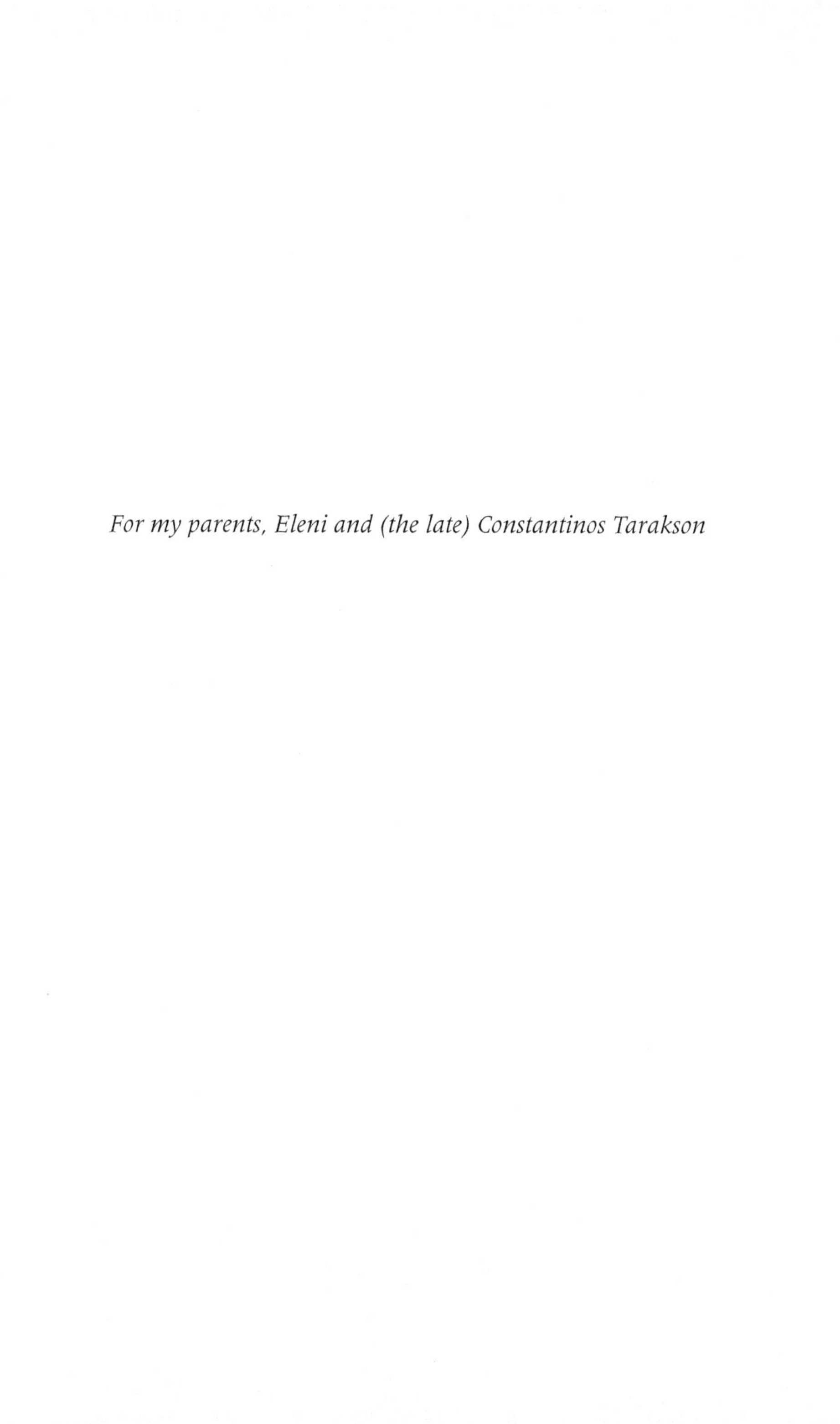

For my parents, Eleni and (the late) Constantinos Tarakson

Contents

Part 4 Securing their futures

Acknowledgments

Many people helped with this book. My thanks must first go to Ian Bowring, Emma Singer and Emma Cotter at Allen & Unwin for making it happen. I would also like to thank the following experts for generously providing information and/or checking accuracy: Jennifer Ames, Acting Director Adoption and Permanent Care Services, Department of Community Services, New South Wales; Australian Bureau of Statistics; Centrelink; Bob Field, Acting General Counsel, Public Trustee, New South Wales; Barbara Minuzzo, community safety consultant, based in Victoria; Frances Neilson, solicitor, Legal Aid Commission, New South Wales; John Powlay, the Private Health Insurance Ombudsman; and Peter Skibinski, husband and prudential regulator.

I would also like to thank AMP and NATSEM (National Centre for Social and Economic Modelling) and the Australian Bureau of Statistics for permitting the reproduction of copyright material.

A special thanks to all those 'other mums' (they know who they are!) who were willing to share their personal experiences, money gripes, and cost cutting hints with me. Although I've got two young children myself, there's nothing like talking to other people who have been there and done that!

Mostly, though, I'd like to thank my parents. Blue-collar Greek migrants, they valued education for their children above all. Requests for books were never declined, so this book is dedicated to them.

Introduction

More and more people are putting off having children well into their thirties, some even into their forties. Money (or the lack of it) is often cited as their reason.

Of course the decision to have kids isn't based primarily on dollars and cents, but there's no denying that the strain on your wallet is enormous. For those used to a dual income the sudden drop when one of you leaves the workforce, if only temporarily, takes getting used to. And for those starting out on a single income, the challenges are even greater.

But it's not as daunting as it sounds.

It's easy to be overwhelmed by monetary matters and lose sight of the bigger issue. Yes, children cost money. But what you gain is beyond measure.

Thankfully there are ways to make the financial aspects of parenthood easier, and help you reach your dream sooner. All it takes is some sensible planning, smart decision making, and knowing where to trim expenses without compromising the health and happiness of your child. That's where *Raising Kids . . . Without Breaking the Bank* can help. Whether you're planning a family or you already have young children, this book will help you make wise financial decisions. From saving up before the birth to ensuring your children's wellbeing beyond your own lifetime—and everything in between. Practical money saving suggestions are offered throughout, always with an eye on safety issues.

Divided into four parts, the structure of this book reflects the natural progression we all go through as parents.

Part 1, 'Planning ahead' stresses the importance of planning. Creating a savings plan, managing your debts, adjusting to one salary and analysing your financial position are among the issues covered in some detail. Also considered are the many costs involved with having a child. How much can you expect to pay in medical fees, and is private health cover all it's cracked up to be? Is IVF or adoption on the cards, and if so how much could you be up for? And how much does it cost to set up the nursery and improve the safety of your home? We look at how to create and use a family budget, the intention being to liberate rather than restrain.

Part 2, 'The early years' examines how you can trim those ongoing expenses—food, clothing, toys, leisure, kids' parties and so forth—without depriving your child of the best you can offer. It also examines the question of going back to work. What are your rights regarding parental leave? Various options are outlined that can help you with the work–family juggling act: such as returning part-time, job sharing and telecommuting. Which of course leads to the issue of childcare, babysitters and nannies. What are your options, how much do they cost, and are there any ways to trim those costs? We even look at ways you can earn an income from home with baby in tow. Part 2 also provides an overview of the relevant forms of government assistance and tax breaks that may well make life easier than you expected.

Part 3, 'As they grow' offers help with the continuing challenges parents face. How much does it cost to educate your child, and is there any help available? Investing for your children's future is something that cannot be taken for granted. Whether it's for their education, a car, help with a home purchase or just a general safety net, you need to find the strategy that's right for you. Part 3 also looks at how you can teach children to save. It's not as impossible as you might think.

Sadly, however, it's also necessary to consider the financial implications of some of the less pleasant life events. You've heard the statistics. Nearly half of all marriages end in divorce. How is child support calculated and would it meet your needs? And what if the worst happens and your partner dies? How can you and your children meet your daily living expenses, particularly in the early days? Which leads us to wills, life insurance and the natural desire we all have to provide for our children even beyond our own lifetimes—all of which is covered in Part 4, 'Securing their futures'.

Please keep in mind that no book can be a substitute for personalised legal or investment advice. When faced with a particular problem or decision always seek expert advice tailored to your situation. At the end of each chapter you will find a section directing you to further help: books, websites, government bodies and other relevant organisations.

Technical terms are kept to a minimum and where jargon is used it is explained simply and clearly. Even so, the glossary at the end of the book provides a handy reference to financial and legal terms. Worksheets, checklists and case studies make this book easy to read and user friendly.

The aim is to help you worry less about money—and focus more of your time on those gummy grins and chubby cheeks.

Part 1

Planning ahead

1

Before you begin

It's a sign of our times. Many of us put off having children because we think we cannot afford them.

Our parents are probably raising their eyebrows in disbelief. 'We raised you on far less money,' they say, 'and you turned out all right.' Maybe so. But our generation has grown up with different expectations. We want to have our sticky date pudding and eat it too. And why not, if it's possible?

It's possible.

All it takes is some smart planning, knowing how to trim costs without compromising your baby's health and happiness, and knowing where to turn for help when necessary.

Children can be expensive, it's true. But what you gain can never be measured in monetary terms. There's simply no correlation between the size of your bank balance and the elation felt when your baby wraps a miniature hand around your finger. Losing sight of the bigger picture can throw the whole issue out of perspective.

We do need to be practical, however. How can we make the financial aspects of parenthood easier? This chapter is a starting point. It helps you assess your current situation, providing a snapshot of where you are right now. It looks at ways to keep debts under control and examines how you can save up for your baby's arrival.

Before you start focusing on the costs of parenthood you need to ask yourself three questions. Where are you now? Where do you want to be by the time you have kids? How will you get there?

Where are you now?

In other words, assess your current situation. This involves setting aside the best part of a quiet day when you have the chance to go through your records and do some serious thinking.

List everything you own and everything you owe. The aim is to estimate how much your assets are worth in today's terms. However, it's not possible to say that if you have over $x, you'll have no financial problems. Neither can you say that if you have under $y you're in strife. So why bother?

Working out your net worth is a starting point on the road to financial security. Not only does it provide a summary of where you are right now, it can help identify steps to improve your position. It may suggest areas where you can cut back on spending, at the same time highlighting a need to build up your investments.

You don't have to be precise. Working out the exact value of your jewellery, antiques, artworks etc. probably requires a professional valuation, and for these purposes is unnecessary—we're really just after something general. Look up your receipts, insurance policies and so on and do some quick research into current prices. For instance, estimate how much your car is worth by checking the prices of comparable cars in the classifieds. For jewellery, antiques and so on, visit a few stores and/or dealers or try surfing the Internet. For personal effects such as furniture, home entertainment etc., be aware that if you had to sell up, secondhand prices are much lower than what you paid. It's those lower prices that you should be recording. Come up with your best guess, photocopy the following worksheet and use it to record your findings. Not all entries will apply to you. Simply ignore those that don't.

Note: superannuation is not included in the worksheet as we're assuming you won't have access to it for many years. This worksheet is for the shorter-term goal of starting a family.

Worksheet 1.1: Assessing your net worth

Assets—what you own
Cash
Cash on hand $__________________
Cash in transaction accounts $__________________
Cash in cheque accounts $__________________
Cash in bonus interest savings accounts $__________________
Other $__________________
TOTAL CASH (a) $__________________

Personal effects
Car, motor bike etc. $__________________
Furniture $__________________
Home entertainment equipment $__________________
Home office equipment $__________________
Appliances $__________________
Tools $__________________
Musical instruments $__________________
Jewellery $__________________
Art $__________________
Antiques $__________________
Collections $__________________
Other $__________________
TOTAL PERSONAL EFFECTS (b) $__________________

Real property
Residence $__________________
Investment property/holiday home $__________________
Property trusts $__________________
TOTAL REAL PROPERTY (c) $__________________

Investments
Term deposits $__________________
Shares $__________________
Managed funds $__________________
Other $__________________
TOTAL INVESTMENTS (d) $__________________

TOTAL ASSETS (a+b+c+d) $__________________

Liabilities—what you owe
Loans
Home loan $__________________

Personal loan	$_______________
Car loan	$_______________
Informal loan (family/friends)	$_______________
Other	$_______________
TOTAL LOANS (i)	$_______________

Current debts

Credit card debt	$_______________
Department store debt	$_______________
Bank overdraft	$_______________
Other	$_______________
TOTAL CURRENT DEBTS (ii)	$_______________

TOTAL LIABILITIES (i+ii)	$_______________

NET WORTH AS OF [*date*_______________]
Total assets – Total liabilities

$_______________

Where do you want to be?

Okay, so it's done. Now you know where you stand. How did you go?

Don't just focus on the total; pay attention to the breakdown. Look at the difference between investments and personal effects. Are you spending too much on consumer goods which, while enjoyable, lose value dramatically once you buy them? Too little on securing your financial future? It's all a matter of balance.

Perhaps you're better off than you expected and there's nothing standing in the way of you starting a family. Sometimes we become overwhelmed when we hear how expensive kids are, and don't realise that we're already in a good enough position to cope. That's not to say that you wouldn't benefit from some smart money-saving moves, which this book can provide. So read on.

Or maybe the figures don't come up to scratch. Maybe your liabilities outweigh your assets, or maybe you're hanging by a thread. Maybe all of your energy is going into the here and now, with little thought for tomorrow. It doesn't mean you should abandon your plans for parenthood. If you have some time up your sleeves, then all the better. If not—don't despair. You can still get there.

How will you get there?

There are steps you can take to improve your financial position before you start a family. These general strategies apply to anyone, and can help those who already have children.

Set goals

Don't flounder in the darkness. Be specific in your ambitions. Sit back down with pen and paper, but this time write down your goals. Divide your sheet into three columns—short-term, intermediate, and long-term.

Maybe starting a family is your most immediate aim, or maybe it's still a few years off. Put it in the appropriate column. What other goals do you have? Do you want to travel? Go on to further study? Start your own business? Retire early? It's important to know what you want to do and when you want to do it.

If possible, work out how much you need to save to meet specific financial goals. Try using one of the online calculators, such as at http://www.btonline.com.au (a quick web search will unearth more). You need to enter your initial deposit, contributions, interest rate, investment period, as well as the rate of inflation.

Prioritise

Not all goals are achievable, regardless of how well we plan and organise. It's a simple fact of human existence that we always want more. Once you've listed your goals, set priorities. Not necessarily for what you want the soonest, but for what you want the most. Look at your list. Decide what to abandon if necessary and what to defer. For instance, can your old car stagger along for a few more years or do you absolutely need a new one now?

Then look at the question from another angle—what is *stopping* you from reaching your goals? It's all well and good to say your goal is to save up for a family, but there might be something stopping you. Do you have massive debts that need to be sorted out first? You may need to set priorities in paying off debts, too. Generally, it's wise to pay off debts for items that fall in value (consumer goods), particularly those that carry high interest rates, such as credit cards.

Budget

'Budget' is a word that makes many people shudder. Budgets sound tedious and time consuming, but they are an excellent tool to help you manage your money. Just the act of creating a budget allows you to identify where you are wasting money and where you can make some savings. See Chapter 5 'The family budget' for step-by-step instructions on how to prepare a budget.

Learn about investing

Leaving your money to slumber in a bank account with virtually no interest isn't going to help you meet your long-term goals. If you've never been into investing, now is the time to learn. Read up about it, and seek the services of a financial planner.

Prepare for the unexpected

Sometimes the unexpected happens. If you are surviving on one income in order to raise young children, what would happen if the earning partner lost their job? If they were fired or made redundant? Redundancy payouts help, of course, but don't last forever. If possible, have a savings pool that you can fall back on until a new job is found. And don't forget to look into government unemployment benefits: call Centrelink on 132 490 for information about payments and eligibility.

Think positive

It's not all hard work and sacrifice. Rather it's a matter of adopting some new habits and trying to get into the swing of things. Be prepared to learn from your mistakes and stay positive.

The long journey

Lauren and Sam had been married for three years when they decided it was time to start a family. Lauren wanted to be an at-home mum, at least until their children started school. It would require her to be out of the workforce for about seven years in total. What they wanted to know was: could they afford it?

Lauren and Sam spent one rainy Sunday working out their net worth. Because their home loan was still quite high, their net worth was lower than they had suspected. They had little money saved. They decided to delay their plans for a child.

Could they live on one income? They agreed to try it out and see.

For the next two years their living expenses came solely from Sam's earnings. It was a challenge at first, but they soon adjusted to the new spending patterns. They used most of Lauren's income in that period to reduce their home loan, placing the remainder in a regular savings plan.

By the end of the two years they had paid off a sizeable chunk of their mortgage. Their savings also improved. They decided to start a family, but recognised that some of Sam's income would then have to go into paying off the home loan and continuing their savings plan.

MANAGING YOUR DEBTS

One of the main obstacles to meeting your financial goals is dealing with existing debts. So how can you avoid such problems arising, and what happens if the problem already exists?

Avoiding debt difficulties

Buying with cash is the cheapest way to go. If you want to use credit or take out a loan, you pay for the privilege and it's much easier to overspend with credit. If you're handing over notes, it's much more obvious how much money is actually going out. It's not always possible to use cash only, however, especially when stocking up for the arrival of a baby.

Credit can be an effective way to spread out payment for costly items, but it can also lead to rapidly mounting debt. You don't need to take to your credit card with a pair of scissors, but you do need to exercise restraint.

Before buying on any credit scheme, look at the full cost—including the cash price, interest, repayments, credit charges and fees. How does it fit in with your other expenses and financial commitments? If you do decide to take the plunge, try to put down as big a cash deposit as possible. This will reduce your repayments and the total interest bill. Be sure to keep copies of all your documentation: quotes, invoices and receipts.

What about taking out a loan? This depends on what you are buying. Department stores, car dealers and so on often offer finance, but before accepting compare their rates to those of banks and other financial institutions. The difference can be significant.

When taking out a loan, be clear about:

- what security is needed for the loan, if any;
- the interest rate;
- the frequency of repayments;
- how much you will actually repay in dollars and cents;
- the term of the loan;
- the fees being charged; and
- whether you can repay the loan early without penalty.

If you're in trouble

Sometimes the unexpected happens and you find yourself unable to pay your debts. The first thing to do is notify the lender as soon as possible. Don't hope they won't notice you've fallen behind on your repayments—because you can bet your bottom dollar that they will.

Try to negotiate a repayment plan that suits both you and your lender. Offer a concrete suggestion that you are confident you can stick to. For instance, you may work out a plan to pay by monthly instalments. Be detailed in your plan, outlining dates and sums. Make sure any agreement reached is in writing.

And what if this doesn't work? What if the lender insists you meet your obligations as originally agreed? If you are suffering hardship, for instance due to illness or unemployment, the Consumer Credit Code gives you the right to apply to court for an order varying the contract. The Code also requires credit providers to be careful not to enter into contracts with people who may find it difficult to meet repayments in the first place.

If you have several debts that are outstanding, one technique often used is debt consolidation. This involves rolling all your debts into one loan, preferably one that has a low interest rate, such as your home loan. It is vital to maintain the repayments on this consolidated loan.

If you find you are facing debt difficulties consult a debt counsellor. If things have gone past the stage of just difficult and entered into the letter from the lawyers' stage, seek legal advice without delay.

SAVINGS STRATEGIES

Here are a few guiding principles when it comes to saving to help you make the most of your money.

The sooner the better

There are two main reasons why it pays to start saving early. The first is the obvious, common-sense one—the earlier you start, the more time you have to reach your goals. Your path won't be such a steep slope, but a somewhat gentler incline.

The other reason relates to compound interest. But what is it exactly? Many of us have vague recollections of those awful equations we had to learn at school, and while we know that compounding works in our favour, we can't quite explain why.

Put simply, compounding works by earning interest on your interest. Rather than just earning interest on the original sum invested (that is, the principal), the interest is reinvested, earning even more interest.

Now for a concrete example.

Tom and Catherine invest $8000 for five years in a deposit account averaging 4 per cent per annum. Let's assume they withdraw the interest and only reinvest the principal (the $8000). In other words, they only earn simple interest. At the end of five years they will have:

Simple interest = principal x rate x number of years
$$= 8000 \times 0.04 \times 5$$
$$= \$1600$$
When they add this to the principal, they will have $9600 in total.

But now let's assume they reinvest the interest and earn interest on it, thus enjoying the benefits of compounding. This sum looks like:

Compound amount = principal x (1 + rate) $^{\text{number of years}}$
$$= 8000 \times (1 + 0.04)^5$$
$$= \$9733.22 \text{ in total}$$
(or interest of $1733.22)

An extra $133.22. The higher the interest rate, the more difference you will notice. And—most importantly—the longer the investment period, the larger the impact. The benefits of compounding are greater where interest is calculated and paid frequently. Does your account pay interest half-yearly, monthly or more often?

Save regularly

The above example looks at what happens to your money when you invest a lump sum. If you make multiple contributions, the benefit is far greater. Even if the regular sum is small, it soon adds up.

The calculations are starting to get complicated, so I'll spare you the hieroglyphics. But let's assume Tom and Catherine start with their initial investment of $8000 and add $50 per month to the account thereafter, again averaging 4 per cent. What would they have after five years?

After five years they would have approximately $13 021.87 (this can vary depending on how you calculate the monthly interest rate)

Not bad, seeing they put in $10 950 all up. Could you manage to put aside $50 per month?

Shop around

Not all financial institutions are equal. When looking for a savings account, be sure to investigate:

- the interest rate;
- how frequently interest is calculated and paid;
- the fees you will be charged;
- how many free transactions you can make per month, and what amounts to a transaction (for example, is an EFTPOS withdrawal considered a transaction);
- whether there is a minimum balance requirement; and
- whether there are minimum deposit requirements and/or restrictions on withdrawals.

SAVINGS OPTIONS

There are various ways you can put money aside to save up for your baby. Some are better than others, and you need to weigh up the pros and cons and decide what best suits your needs.

Ordinary savings account

This is the simplest option. Open an account with a bank/ building society/credit union, and start saving. You might want to create a separate account dedicated solely to meeting your goal. Avoid using the money for any other purpose if possible.

Bonus interest accounts

Many financial institutions offer bonus interest accounts to encourage savings. Usually, these accounts can still be used as ordinary transaction accounts (good in an emergency) but if you treat them that way you may lose the benefit of the higher interest rate. For example, your account might attract bonus interest in a given month if you make at least one deposit but no withdrawals in that month.

Term deposits

Traditionally term deposits offer better interest rates than trans-action and bonus interest accounts. Be sure to check this for yourself, however, as trends can change. Normally you need a significant sum to open a term deposit. This can be $1000 in some cases, but some institutions require a higher figure such as $5000.

Term deposits are less flexible than ordinary accounts. If for some reason you need to withdraw money before the term expires you will face a penalty. This may not be a bad thing. It helps you avoid the temptation to dip into the funds until maturity. Decide when you need to have access to the money—for example when your baby is due or a short time prior—and match the maturity date to your needs.

Internet savings accounts

Financial institutions are starting to offer higher interest Internet savings accounts. These operate electronically or through call centres and need to be linked with a transaction account. For daily expenditures you generally use the low interest transaction account, while you sweep your excess funds into the Internet account.

Shifting money around can lead to extra transactions (and perhaps extra fees) and the need to be more alert as to how much money you have in each account at any given time. Even so, the higher interest rate often makes it worthwhile, particularly if you're building up a strong stable balance. You may be able to make use of automatic savings plans where nominated sums are transferred, which saves you having to shift the money around yourself.

Cash management trusts

Cash management trusts are run by funds managers who invest on behalf of unit holders. These trusts are typically confined to highly liquid securities such as bank deposits and short-term government paper. Check this, however, because some go beyond these into areas that could potentially increase the risk of loss.

Returns tend to be higher than ordinary savings accounts because investment money is pooled, giving access to the wholesale short-term money market. This means you earn money-market interest, but keep in mind you need to pay fees to the fund manager.

Minimum balances apply and can be rather high—typically $5000. High minimum withdrawal requirements tend to make these unsuitable for day-to-day transactions. Some are more flexible than others, however, and you need to determine your requirements before you choose. A withdrawal requires the redemption of units, with the money then generally being transferred into your bank transaction account. This means you often can't get same-day access to the funds. Before investing in any managed fund read the product disclosure statement carefully and compare products offered by various funds managers.

Cash management accounts

Similar to cash management trusts, but in this case run by banks. Here the banks set the interest rate, as opposed to you receiving what the fund earns minus fees. Another difference is that banks are required to hold capital against the investments they make with the deposits, while funds managers aren't.

As cash management accounts are a bank deposit, you can generally get access to the funds on a same-day basis. Typical minimum balances are $1000, $2000 or $5000. You may need to have a fairly high balance before you enjoy the benefits of higher interest rates. Again, make sure you have a thorough understanding of the product before you invest.

Other

You'll notice there's been no mention of shares or property. That's because these types of investments are usually considered to be medium- to long-term—say, five to ten years or more. You probably want to start a family before that. But if you do have that much time up your sleeve and want to look at these options as a type of saving for kids strategy you can refer to Chapter 13, 'Securing your children's financial future'. As the title suggests, it looks at ways you can build wealth for your family's future. The information applies equally to any medium- to long-term wealth creation goal.

FURTHER HELP

- The 'money manager' website provides information on personal finance issues. Part of the Fairfax Interactive Network, it's associated with various newspapers and finance magazines. It allows you to compare accounts online and provides general information on banking, saving, and debt management. See http://www.moneymanager.com.au.
- The Australian Bankers' Association provides information on banking related matters such as selecting the right savings account and choosing a loan. See http://www.bankers.asn.au.
- For information on the uniform Consumer Credit Code, a law that regulates creditors' and debtors' rights and obligations throughout Australia, see http://www.creditcode.gov.au or contact the department of fair trading/consumer affairs in your state.
- If you have problems with debt you can contact the Credit Helpline in your state (see the *White Pages*).

Useful publications

Ingram, A. and O'Donnell, P. 2002, *My Money, My Self*, Choice Books, Sydney.

Jakobi, H. 2001, *Financial Freedom . . . Starting Now!*, Wealth Dynamics International, Portland.

James, V. 2003, *The Woman's Money Book*, revised edn, Allen & Unwin, Sydney.

Sampson, A. 2000, *The Money Book*, Allen & Unwin, Sydney.

2

Medical costs

When someone asks you how much it costs to have children, what do you instantly think of? The costs of setting up the nursery, perhaps? Or maybe the ongoing costs of food, clothing and, eventually, education? Or maybe you focus more on the lost income that results from not being able to work for a while. All valid considerations, of course, but all overlooking something important.

Often we forget to factor in how much it costs to actually have the baby in the first place. In other words, the medical costs associated with the pregnancy and the birth. Depending on your choices, these can be virtually zero or somewhere in the thousands.

This chapter looks at the medical costs involved with having a baby—both when things run smoothly and when falling pregnant turns out to be harder than expected. Central to the whole issue is the question of private health insurance compared to the public health system. Should you run for cover?

PRENATAL AND BIRTHING CARE

When it comes to being pregnant and giving birth, we all have similar fears and hopes. We want the pregnancy to be trouble free, the birth to be as painless as possible and the baby to be healthy.

But our views on the type of prenatal and birthing care we desire diverge dramatically. Some women feel comforted by the technological resources of a hospital; others prefer the homey atmosphere of birth centres or their own homes. Some prefer the ongoing care of the obstetrician of their choice; others prefer the services of midwives. Some favour a drug-free natural birth; others cry 'Epidural!' as soon as they set foot in the delivery room. There's a lot that goes into forming your views—your upbringing, cultural background, previous experience, medical condition. And of course your financial position.

Your options

Putting money matters aside for the moment, what are your options for prenatal and birthing care? Depending on where you live, some of the following options may not be available.

Obstetrician

You may opt for specialist obstetric care, where you choose your own obstetrician. He or she orders all the necessary tests such as blood tests and ultrasounds, and keeps tabs on the results. If all goes well you would see that obstetrician about once a month to begin with, then at around six to seven months you would go once a fortnight. As the birth approaches you may be required to go once a week. The obstetrician usually attends the birth (although this is not guaranteed) and is responsible for your post partum care. Six weeks or so after the birth you go back for a follow-up examination.

People selecting their own obstetrician usually have private health insurance, although this is not a prerequisite. You may be able to choose to go to a private hospital or book in as a private patient in a public hospital. You can select between a birth centre, where the emphasis is on natural drug-free processes, and a traditional labour ward. The obstetrician can discuss the merits of each with you.

Hospital staff

If you decide to have your baby under the public health system, a midwife or doctor appointed by the hospital is responsible for your care. You cannot choose who you use. Again, you may be able to select between a birth centre and labour ward. When things run smoothly, midwives may provide most of the care, but doctors are on hand should problems arise.

Shared care

You might be able to see your GP for frequent regular check ups, and only go to an obstetrician or midwife periodically. This might be an attractive option for women in isolated communities, especially in regions where maternity wards are closing. These women have to travel long distances, sometimes 100 km or more, to get to their nearest hospital or visit their specialist. On top of all the other costs add petrol, wear and tear on their motor vehicle, possible accommodation expenses if they need to stay overnight, and the cost of losing a whole day's work to visit their hospital.

Independent midwife

Some midwives run their own practice. They can provide care during the entire pregnancy, birth and post birth, or you can choose to use them for selected purposes only. The setting can be your own home or in a hospital/birth centre that they are attached to. In the past, they could act as the main caregiver during a hospital or birth centre delivery. Now, due to the ubiquitous insurance problems, they may only act as an independent support person while staff midwives provide the midwifery services.

The costs

You can probably guess which is the cheapest. Having a baby in a public hospital as a public patient is free. Under the Medicare system, all Australians are entitled to free treatment in public hospitals, irrespective of their insurance status. There may still be some costs for public patients, for example if you see a GP who does not bulk bill. Various diagnostic tests, such as ultrasounds, may also not be bulk billed. In these situations you might end up paying a few hundred dollars over the course of the pregnancy.

If you want to choose your own obstetrician, you pay for the privilege. How much? It all depends on the doctor. The

Australian Medical Association has scheduled fees, but doctors are at liberty to charge well above them, and many do.

Fees have undergone a significant hike in recent years, largely due to the professional indemnity insurance crisis. If you had your first child a few years ago and are now planning your second, be prepared to hear a much higher figure quoted.

At the time of writing, the Medicare rebate was $25.70 per prenatal visit, but you are likely to be charged considerably more than that. Even if your pregnancy goes well, you can still expect to need ten or so prenatal visits. If there are complications or yours is a high-risk pregnancy, expect to go more often. Add the costs of the delivery itself and post partum care: $1000 to $4000 or even more. The Medicare rebate varies depending on the services performed and whether there were any complications. At the time of writing, the rebate for the most commonly claimed items plus five days post partum care was $332.70. Rebate figures are re-adjusted each November. Health insurance coverage varies depending on your policy.

Ancillary costs abound for private patients. You may need to pay for medical tests including blood tests, glucose tolerance tests, ultrasounds, amniocentesis tests and so forth. Some may be bulk billed, meaning the provider accepts the Medicare rebate as full payment. Often you need to pay the difference between the charge and the Medicare rebate yourself. Depending on what needs to be done, tests can end up costing you a few hundred dollars. If you use an anaesthetist, for instance for an epidural, you may need to pay the anaesthetist directly. This can also be a few hundred dollars. You might need to pay a proportion of the hospital's fees. These are separate from the fees charged by the obstetrician. Whether you need to pay this depends on your health fund.

So how much can it cost a private patient all up? By the time you factor in obstetrician's fees and ancillary charges, a sum of $3000 to $5000 out of your personal pocket is not unreasonable. If you don't have private cover and you want to go down the private trail, you'll be paying in the vicinity of $8000 to $10 000. If complications occur, fees can be even higher.

The other option discussed above was independent midwife

care. On average midwives charge between $2500 and $4000, depending on their experience and the number of women they are caring for. Medicare does not refund any of this, although some health funds do provide a small amount of cover.

Keep in mind that fee levels change and you should do your own research before making a final decision.

ASSISTED CONCEPTION

Say you've been trying to fall pregnant for a considerable length of time without success. More than a year has passed. You've both had the necessary medical tests and your doctor recommends you consider assisted conception. It sounds daunting, but you're open to learning more about it.

There are various options, which you would of course discuss with your doctor. Your GP can provide you with a referral to a fertility clinic. Make sure you do get a referral, because they are needed for claiming Medicare rebates. After you make an appointment with the clinic you usually go in for an interview, where they explain the full picture and you're able to make an informed decision.

Let's assume you decide to go ahead. How much will this cost you?

The costs

The fertility centre or clinic will be able to give you detailed information about costs, including the ability to claim money back from Medicare and/or your health fund. You will also need to contact your health fund to discover exactly what is claimable and what isn't.

Unfortunately, it is very hard to generalise about assisted conception costs. It all depends on the precise nature and extent of the treatment as well as how much the individual clinic chooses to charge. Success may or may not be rapid; chances are you will go through several attempts before getting pregnant. Each attempt costs more money. You won't know how many times it's necessary until you go through it yourself.

I'm reluctant to give even a general guideline as to costs. The clinics themselves can't provide me with generic estimates and claim it is misleading for me to even try. Suffice it to say that if you are considering in vitro fertilisation (IVF) or one of its variants you will be paying in the thousands of dollars. In the end you might have a baby or you might not. Nobody can decide for you whether it is worth the risks and the costs. That is something only you can decide.

Help with the costs

At least it's possible to provide some general cost saving tips. These tips apply to medical treatment in general, not just assisted conception.

Medicare Safety Net

Medicare normally rebates 85 per cent of the government set Medicare schedule fee for outpatient services and 75 per cent for private inpatient services.

The difference between this payment and the Medicare schedule fee is the gap amount. Once your gap payments reach a set figure within a calendar year you are eligible for the Safety Net. At the time of writing, the figure was $328 but this is readjusted each January. Medicare benefits then increase to 100 per cent of the Medicare schedule fee for further services that year.

But don't be confused. If your provider charges more than the Medicare schedule fee (and many do), that extra amount does not count towards the Safety Net.

Presentation of receipts is required. Individuals don't need to register for the Safety Net, but families and couples do. To register, complete a Safety Net Registration Form, available through all Medicare branches. Backdating is not possible and the benefit only commences from the date you register, so the sooner you do it, the better.

Proposed MedicarePlus Safety Net

Under new proposals to modify Medicare (known as Medicare-Plus), various reforms have been put forward, including a new Safety Net.

For Concession Card holders and families receiving Family Tax Benefit Part A, the government proposes to cover 80 per cent of out-of-pocket costs for medical services outside hospital above $500 per individual or family per year. For all others, it proposes to cover 80 per cent of out-of-pocket costs for medical services outside hospital above $1000 per individual or family per year.

At the time of writing, these reforms have not yet passed into law.

Pharmaceutical Benefits Scheme (PBS) Safety Net

If you spend a certain amount on PBS medicines in a calendar year (currently $726.80) you can take advantage of the PBS Safety Net, where you are entitled to further PBS medicines at a reduced cost for the remainder of the calendar year. The threshold for pensioner concession card holders is lower (currently $197.60), then further PBS medicines are free for the rest of the calendar year. Safety Net figures are re-adjusted each January.

If you choose the more expensive brand alternatives, the extra amount does not count towards the Safety Net.

Apply through your pharmacist. If you use the same pharmacist each time they may be able to keep records of your spending. If you use several ask for a prescription record form, which you hand over each time.

Not all drugs used for assisted conception are eligible, but it's worth looking in to.

Net medical expenses tax offset

The net medical expenses tax offset (previously known as a rebate) may be available if you have out-of-pocket medical expenses over a set sum in a given financial year. Currently the sum is $1250 but legislation before parliament might, if passed, increase the threshold to $1500.

Keep in mind the offset is for net expenses—the amount you paid less any refunds received from Medicare or health funds. Payments for IVF procedures are included.

PRIVATE HEALTH INSURANCE

Private health insurance is discussed in this chapter because it impacts directly on the costs of having a baby. But its relevance to parents goes far beyond that. Most people don't take out private cover just to get them through childbirth and then opt out again. For many, it's an ongoing expense intended to apply to many situations, particularly to deal with the medical costs of a growing family.

As you are no doubt aware, the costs of health insurance have been rising steadily in recent years. Many families are starting to ask whether it's all worth it.

The pros and cons

Apart from financial aspects, there are three key advantages to private health insurance. The first is queue jumping for elective surgery. Under the public system, the wait can be months for non-urgent and semi-urgent cases. With private cover, the wait may be shorter. There may still be some wait, however, as more people join the private system.

With private cover you have access to private hospitals, which may well be too expensive to contemplate without insurance. They're generally more lavish than public hospitals.

Another advantage is the ability to select your own doctor. When you are undertaking a complex procedure or where you are receiving care on a long-term regular basis (for instance when having a baby), it can be comforting to have the doctor of your choice.

Then again, we can chip away at these advantages.

Queue jumping does not apply to emergencies, where everyone is treated in accordance with their medical condition. And you might end up in a public hospital rather than a private one anyway—for instance in an emergency or where special equipment is required. As for the ability to select your own doctor, often there's no guarantee that your obstetrician, for example, will be there to deliver your baby.

Waiting periods generally apply, meaning a certain time must elapse before the benefits are available. If you are contemplating starting a family and want to take out private cover specifically for that purpose, check to see whether there is a waiting period before you can claim.

Now for money matters. Premiums have been rising steadily and will probably continue to do so. Some commentators speculate that you would be better off saving the premiums and investing them, then drawing on that money when you need to pay for medical treatment. Whether that is actually so is a matter for debate. The thing is, nobody can predict what the future will bring. You may have little need for treatment, and feel ripped off. Or you may need a great deal. Who knows?

With private cover you may end up having significant out-of-pocket expenses anyway, whereas under Medicare treatment is free.

The government has introduced financial incentives to encourage people to take out private cover (see below). These incentives might sway your decision; they might not.

A tale of two mothers

Maria was a member of a health fund for several years, shelling out for the premiums and rarely claiming. Until she got pregnant. Her obstetrician didn't have links with a private hospital, so she ended up having her baby in a public hospital as a private patient. She didn't get her own room, which she had previously believed she was entitled to. The woman she shared a room with was a public patient who received identical care to Maria, even down to having the same doctor for the delivery. Her neighbour paid zero dollars. Maria was out of pocket about $3000 on top of all the premiums she'd been steadily paying. Not surprisingly, she was dissatisfied with the private health system and no longer believed it was worthwhile.

In contrast, Kim was happy. Her son hurt his knee during sports training. Not requiring urgent attention, the injury was classified as elective surgery. Under the public system, there would have been a wait of several months and her son was in considerable pain. With private cover they jumped the queue and had the operation performed with minimum delay.

TYPES OF COVER

If you do decide to take out private health insurance, what level of cover do you need? Basic hospital cover? Or should you go for a broader family policy that includes ancillary items such as glasses, dental treatment, orthodontic braces and so forth?

The choice is not straightforward. Many health funds offer different levels of extras cover ranging from basic ancillary costs (dental, optical) to broader ranges of services with higher benefits. If you do decide on cover for extras, where should you draw the line? And do you want to include cover for 'lifestyle' expenses such as swimming lessons and sports equipment? What about natural therapies? Generally, the higher the depth and breadth of cover, the greater the premium.

Having an idea of how much treatment can cost might help you make your decision. These figures are very general, of course, but when it comes to growing children you can expect to pay about:

- $100 to $180 for a routine half-yearly visit to the dentist, which includes a check up, clean and fluoride treatment;
- $80 to $180 for a filling;
- $5000 for upper and lower orthodontic braces;
- $100 to $300 for a pair of glasses;
- $40 to $50 per half hour speech therapy session;
- $40 to $50 per physiotherapy session; and
- $80 for the meningococcal vaccine, before free treatment recently became available.

One of the things to examine when shopping around is how much the health funds refund for particular items. To put it another way, how much still needs to come out of your pocket?

It's hard to know in advance what your family's actual needs will be. Your children might have perfect teeth and eyesight, or you might find yourself paying several thousands of dollars over the years for medical and dental problems.

The important thing is to be alert. If your dentist spots the early signs indicating braces will be required in the years to come, you might decide to take out appropriate cover when the time is right, keeping waiting periods in mind. Similarly, if your preschool/daycare detects a potential speech problem, start preparing by looking into the costs of cover for speech pathology.

GOVERNMENT SURCHARGES AND INCENTIVES

The government is keen for people to join private health funds, taking some of the pressure off the public purse. Various incentives exist to encourage you to sign on the dotted line. Currently these include:

Medicare levy surcharge

The Medicare levy surcharge is a 1 per cent surcharge on taxable income in addition to the normal 1.5 per cent Medicare levy paid by most taxpayers.

The Medicare levy surcharge aims to encourage high income earners to take out private hospital cover. You are considered a high income earner if you have an annual taxable income over $50 000 (for singles) or $100 000 (for families and couples). The family threshold goes up by $1500 for each dependent child after the first.

Is this you? If so, you'll be slugged with the levy surcharge if you don't have appropriate hospital cover. Extras such as dental and optical are okay but they can't be the sole basis of cover. Your excess must be equal to or less than $500 per annum for single policies or $1000 for family/couples policies.

Lifetime health cover

If you take out hospital cover before you turn 31 you'll pay lower premiums throughout your life compared to those joining later. People joining later will have to pay a 2 per cent loading on top of their premium for every year they are aged over 30. The older you are when you join, the more it'll cost. Someone delaying joining until age 40 will pay 20 per cent more than a person joining at age 30.

Thirty per cent rebate

For every dollar you contribute to your private health insurance premium, the government will give you back 30 cents. This is regardless of the level of cover or the type of membership.

The rebate is payable in one of three ways:

- in the form of reduced premiums;
- as a direct payment from Medicare; or
- as a lump sum claimed back on your tax return.

Gap cover

For medical services inside hospitals (as a private patient) Medicare covers 75 per cent of the government set Medicare schedule fee, with the health fund covering the remaining 25 per cent. A gap arises when doctors charge more than the Medicare schedule fee. Typically, you need to pay the gap yourself.

The gap may be covered by your health fund if there is an agreement or gap cover scheme involving the fund, the hospital and the doctor. It is important to check with your health fund and doctor as not all providers participate in this scheme.

CHOOSING A POLICY

Choosing a fund is never easy. There are so many out there, all offering different variations on a basic theme thus making it hard to compare them directly. The following checklist can help you work your way through the maze.

Health fund checklist

Start by asking yourself a few basic questions:

- What type of cover do you need (hospital, ancillaries or combination)?
- Regarding hospital cover, do you want top cover, tailored cover, or basic cover?

- Regarding ancillaries, which services do you want covered (dental, optical, natural therapies etc.)?
- How much of an excess are you willing to pay?
- How much are you prepared to pay for premiums?

Once you know what you can afford and what you desire, choose a few health funds and ask them:

- What treatments are covered and what is excluded?
- What are the waiting periods?
- What benefit levels are paid and how do I qualify?
- What limits apply?
- How many times does the excess apply per year?
- Which doctors and hospitals do you have agreements with?
- What types of out-of-pocket expenses will I face?
- When did you last raise your premiums?

For a small fee, you can view an Australian Consumers' Association (Choice) report on their website. It allows you to work out what you want and what you are prepared to pay, to compare products and use online calculators. See http://www.choice.com.au.

PRUNING THE PREMIUMS

There are ways to cut the costs of your health insurance premiums. Keep in mind, however, that saving money today could cost you more tomorrow. It's hard to predict, as you don't know what the future will bring—so decide carefully.

You can cut back on the costs of private cover by:

- Buying a policy that limits or excludes some treatments.
- Accepting a high excess. This is an amount payable upfront to the hospital or other provider. It may be a fixed amount each time treatment is received, or a set amount payable per year, or a combination.
- Entering a co-payment deal, meaning you pay an agreed amount, usually per day of treatment. For instance you

might agree to pay a certain amount for each day that you stay in a hospital.

- Taking out a policy that only covers you as a private patient in a public hospital (not in a private hospital).
- Taking out a policy before turning 31 or as soon as possible after that. You can buy the cheapest cover there is and still qualify for the lifetime health cover incentive.

AVOIDING PROBLEMS

The Private Health Insurance Ombudsman is an independent body that resolves complaints between consumers and their health fund. If, after attempting to resolve the problem directly with the fund, you find that you need extra help, you can call the Ombudsman on 1800 640 695 anywhere in Australia.

The Ombudsman has released a list of 'ten golden rules'—ten hints to help you pick the right health fund and avoid problems further down the line.

1. Read the fine print.
2. Check waiting periods. Not just when you apply to join, but when you upgrade your cover.
3. Check if benefit limitation periods apply. These effectively impose additional waiting periods for benefits above the default amount.
4. Contact your fund to confirm cover before you enter hospital.
5. Review cover regularly to ensure it keeps meeting your needs.
6. Keep payments up to date or risk cancellation.
7. When switching to a new fund, check you don't need to re-serve the waiting period.
8. Lodge claims promptly to avoid refusal of payout.
9. Understand how limits, excesses and co-payments are calculated.
10. Take out separate cover while overseas.

Source: Summarised from a more comprehensive article on the Private Health Insurance Ombudsman's website at http://www.phio.org.au, with the kind permission of the Ombudsman.

FURTHER HELP

- For information on private midwives call your state's branch of the Australian Society of Independent Midwives (see the *White Pages*). You can also visit the website of Maternity Coalition, an umbrella consumer advocacy organisation. See http://www.maternitycoalition.org.au.
- For further details regarding assisted conception see the Australian Fertility Society's website at http://www.fsa.au.com or call 03 9645 6359. Also worth visiting is the Australian National Infertility Network's website at http://www.access.org.au.
- For details of Medicare rebates and safety nets see the Health Insurance Commission's website at http://www.hic.gov.au or call Medicare on 132 011.
- For information on most government incentives for private health insurance see the website of the Commonwealth Department of Health and Aged Care at http://www.health.gov.au.
- At the time of writing, the federal government unveiled proposed reforms to Medicare, packaged as the 'MedicarePlus' reforms. For details about the proposal, visit the Department of Health and Ageing's website at http://www.health.gov.au or call 1800 011 163.
- For information regarding the Medicare Levy Surcharge or the Medical Expenses Tax Offset call the Australian Taxation Office on 132 861 or visit http://www.ato.gov.au.
- Visit the Private Health Insurance Administration Council's website for details of all gap cover schemes currently in operation. The council is an independent statutory authority that regulates the private health insurance industry. See http://www.phiac.gov.au.

Useful publications

Public Health Insurance Administration Council, 2001, *Insure? Not Sure? Your Quick Guide to Private Health Insurance.*

3

Adopting a child

For many couples, adopting a child is the only way to realise their dream of starting a family. Others see it as the perfect way to augment their existing family. Whatever your motivation, the decision to adopt is one that can never be taken lightly. Everybody's interests must be taken into account, most particularly those of the child to be adopted. In all cases, the child's wellbeing is the paramount consideration.

Both partners must agree to the adoption, as must any existing children who are old enough to have an opinion. It will make your life easier if your extended family and friendship network is also supportive of your decision. If you're currently undertaking infertility treatment, the adoption agency may advise you to wait until the treatment is completed before you consider adopting a child.

So if after considerable soul searching you decide to go ahead, what do you need to do? And, as the focus of this book is on money, how much will it cost?

THE PROCEDURES

All adoptions must be arranged through official channels. In Australia, trying to arrange an adoption outside of these channels is illegal.

Adoption legislation is state based, as are adoption programs. The first step is to contact your state's community or family services department, or a government-authorised private adoption agency. If desired, the department can provide details of private agencies in your area. They may include Anglicare, Centacare (Catholic Welfare Australia) and Barnardos.

Once you have selected an agency, ask them to send you an information package and the relevant forms.

You may be required to attend seminars and preparation programs. These will help give you an insight into what is involved, as well as explaining procedural matters in more detail.

Once you decide you're ready to take the plunge, your suitability as an adoptive parent will be assessed. The screening and interviewing process is lengthy and intensive. Some people consider it intrusive. It may be stressful, but keep in mind that a child's wellbeing is at stake.

Prospective parents wanting to adopt are required to meet criteria that include providing information about their:

- character and background;
- mental and physical health;
- age and maturity;
- income and finances;
- marital status and family network;
- reasons for wanting to adopt;
- religion;
- child rearing philosophy;
- willingness to discuss the adoption with the child; and
- any other matters relevant to their ability to provide a good home for the adoptive child.

The assessment process can take a few months to complete.

Once you are finally approved, you will have to wait for placement. Waiting times vary between programs. You will have learnt about this during your preparation program. The process can take a dishearteningly long time, particularly if you want to adopt a baby. If you are prepared to adopt an older child or a child with special needs, the wait might (but not necessarily) be shorter. Then again, the challenges involved with raising such a child may well be greater. It may be a long wait, but the emphasis is on placing the right child with the right family.

When a child eventually becomes available, you may not be able to make a formal adoption application immediately. First, you might need to go through a trial period where the child lives with you and the situation is monitored carefully. When you and the child settle into your new life and things are working out you can make your application for formal approval.

This trial period does not always apply, for instance in the case of adoptions of children from countries where the Hague Convention on Inter-country Adoptions applies. The Convention establishes safeguards and minimum standards of care. Where an overseas adoption is from a non-signatory country, the supervision period may apply.

When the formal adoption is eventually granted you take over all the legal rights and responsibilities of the natural parents.

YOUR OPTIONS

Adopting a baby is not your only option, although it's the one most people first consider. You may also want to think about the following alternatives.

Older children

The wait to adopt an older child might be less than the wait for a baby. There are extra considerations, however, that need to be addressed. Older children may have bonds with their natural parents or a foster family, and may find it hard to settle down with you. You need to decide whether you are capable of meeting the challenge and work out how you would handle such problems. Families are chosen for placement based on the needs of the child and the skills the adoptive family will bring to parenting an older child.

Children with special needs

Here we are talking about children with emotional problems and/or physical and intellectual disabilities. You will have to demonstrate that you are capable of meeting these needs. If the child has a wheelchair, for instance, you may be obliged to install ramps and other facilitating devices. Can you learn to meet the requirements of a child who has special developmental needs?

Overseas children

Due to the scarcity of babies available for adoption at home, many people consider adopting a child from overseas. You not only need to satisfy Australian adoption and immigration laws, you also need to meet the laws in the baby's country of origin.

The procedure is much more complicated and far more expensive. There is a lot more involved, including the need to organise a passport and visa and sort out citizenship issues. You need to sponsor the child, meaning you agree to support him or her. You are required to travel to the country to collect the child.

Let the adoption agency know which country you prefer. You might desire the country of your own family's origin, but that choice might not be available. Not all countries have compatible laws. If you have no preference or your choice is unavailable, the agency can provide you with a list of possible countries. The adoption agency then approaches these countries on your behalf.

The older the child, the more difficult it becomes for them to adjust to a new country. Obviously it's easier if you have the same cultural or racial background as the child. If not, think it through carefully. Are you prepared to integrate aspects of the child's culture into your home life? Will you be able to explain cultural differences to the child and provide loving support if he or she experiences racism? Learn as much as possible about your child's country of origin to help make the transition smoother.

Stepchildren and other relatives

If you are considering adopting your stepchildren or other relatives (such as nieces or nephews), the system is quite different.

You (the applicant adoptive parent) must have cared for the child for at least five years. The court must be satisfied that other possible court orders, from either the Family Court or Children's Court, will not meet the child's needs.

Where the non-adoptive natural parent is still alive it might be necessary to have his or her consent. If this person cannot be found or has abdicated responsibility for the child, their consent might not be needed.

The motives and considerations behind this type of adoption are also different. A stepfather might simply want the child to have his surname, but there are other ways to achieve this. Keep in mind that if adopted, the child's legal relationship with their extended family on the side of the non-adoptive parent is severed.

Laws vary between states, but generally you need to make a court application. The department of family or community services may be required to prepare a report to the court. Legal advice should be sought if you are considering an intra family adoption.

THE COSTS

Now we come down to the nitty gritty. How much will it cost to adopt a child? Different agencies have different set fees and these need to be checked with the actual agency.

As an illustration, the New South Wales Department of Community Services charges $3600 for a local adoption. This covers the:

- lodgement of the application;
- costs of attending the seminars;
- assessment reports;
- placement fees;
- court costs; and
- legal fees.

Let me just emphasise that the adoption costs are for various types of fees. It doesn't mean you are actually buying the baby!

The costs for an overseas adoption are significantly higher. All of the above apply, plus extras. Legal and assessment fees are charged by both countries. Documents sent overseas need to be notarised, legalised, and authenticated. Translation fees may also be charged. And don't forget you need to allow for travel and accommodation costs when you go overseas to pick up the child. Costs can be between $10 000 and $30 000, depending on the program in the child's country of origin.

Intra-family adoption costs could be around the $2000 to $2500 mark. This includes the:

- court application fee;
- social worker's report;
- documentation; and
- legal fees.

The exact amount of the legal fees depends on how much your lawyer charges and different lawyers have different rates. If the case is contested, charges will be significantly higher.

Dream finally comes true

Robyn and Richard wanted a child above all other things. After a year of trying, they discovered they had fertility difficulties. They spent a couple of years (and several thousands of dollars) attempting assisted conception. Dishearteningly, they did not succeed.

Eventually they decided to adopt. They went through the appropriate processes. Although keen to start a family, they recognised the realities and knew they had to wait until the right child was placed with them. They spent the time saving money to make up for the high cost they had already expended on assisted conception, and to allow them to better provide for their child when he or she arrived.

Finally, several years after they first started trying for a child, their dream came true. For them, it was worth the outlay and the wait.

FURTHER HELP

- For information about adoption procedures, contact the department of family or community services in your state or talk to a private authorised adoption agency.
- For information on adopting overseas children, see the Department of Immigration and Multicultural and Indigenous Affairs' website at http://www.immi.gov.au.

Useful publications

Department of Immigration and Multicultural and Indigenous Affairs 2002, 'Child migration'.

Reader's Digest (Australia) Pty Ltd (ed.), 1999, *Easy Guide to Your Rights in Australia*, Reader's Digest, Sydney.

Also, each state and territory in Australia has a version of *The Law Handbook*, produced by various legal services/centres, providing a good overview of the law.

4

Setting up

Setting up your home is one of the most enjoyable aspects of expecting a baby. Few things put you into nesting mode more than browsing through rows of lace-edged cot sheets and soft little blankets. Just be careful it doesn't also put you into spending mode.

Setting up is expensive, there's no doubt about that. You can easily end up spending a few thousand dollars before the baby even arrives. Fortunately there are ways you can trim the costs without depriving yourself or your baby of the best you can offer. Many new parents buy items that they don't need, simply because they lack the experience to know what is necessary and what is not.

Experienced parents, on the other hand, know there's a great deal you can do without. Some things aren't necessary, others you can work around.

But before you hit the shops keep in mind that there's something far more important than costs here. Safety. Beware of cutting corners that could put your child at risk. This chapter looks at ways you can save money without compromising your child's safety. It also examines the costs of improving the safety of your home.

SAFETY ISSUES

This book focuses on money. Safety issues are raised as it would be irresponsible to omit them, but there is no way to make an in-depth analysis in a book of this sort. Please research these matters thoroughly before you buy.

The first step is to see if Australian Standards have been met. Compliance ensures adherence to minimum safety and design requirements. Is there a label attached to the product saying that it complies with a particular standard? Check with the store staff if you have any concerns. Keep in mind that standards are compulsory for some products, such as new household cots, but only voluntary for others, such as strollers.

Websites of bodies such as the Child Accident Prevention Foundation of Australia (Kidsafe) and the Ministerial Council on Consumer Affairs provide important guidelines that allow you to make wise purchase decisions. See 'Further help' at the end of this chapter.

But choosing a safe product is not the end of the story. Don't assume all will be well: product usage and maintenance are also important—for example, slinging shopping bags on the back of a stroller can cause it to tip over. The above websites also provide tips for the safe use of baby products.

WHAT DO YOU NEED?

The list is long and the options are endless. What starts as a fun shopping trip soon takes on the proportions of a mountain trek when you realise how much there is to buy. Don't try to tackle everything at once. You'll only become overwhelmed, which leads to poor purchase decisions.

The following worksheet makes shopping around easier. Photocopy the pages and take them with you. Where helpful, a typical price or price range has been included in the worksheet. If not, it means that prices vary so markedly a guide wouldn't help. For instance you can buy cot blankets for as little as $20 or you can pay into the low hundreds. It depends on the material, style, country of origin and so on. Prices also vary between stores, brands and models.

Record your findings in the worksheet's research section and enter your final choice in the last column. This makes it easy to add up all the entries and see if your budget allows for the purchases.

Don't assume you need to buy everything listed. Read the section 'What don't you need?' (page 42) and if you decide to forgo something, cross it off your worksheet.

You'll notice toys, clothes and formula/food aren't listed. For information, see Chapter 6, 'Ongoing costs'.

Worksheet 4.1— Shopping for baby

Item	Typical price	Research	Final choice
Nursery			
Cot	$240–800 (av. $550)		
Cot mattress	$50 foam, $100 inner sprung		
Cot sheets			
Cot blanket			
Bassinette	$150–400		
Bedding and mattress for bassinette	$100		
Change table	$50 folding, $200 wooden		
Change mat	$30		
Lotions/wipes/ bath bubbles/ shampoo			
Bathroom			
Baby bath	$20–50		
Towels, face washers			
Nappy bucket	$15		
Nappy bin	$50		
Potty	$50 fancy, $7 basic		
Kitchen			
High chair	$100–300		
Bottle steriliser	$150 plug-in, $60 microwave, $25 Milton Steriliser		
Breast pump, manual	$40–100		
Bottles			
Plates, bowls			
Training cups			
Bibs			

Going out
Pram
Layback stroller $150–400
Upright stroller $40–100
Jogger stroller $250–800
Pram blanket
Rain cover
Sunshade/mozzie net
Nappy bag $40–120
Portable change mat
Baby sling $35–150
Travel cot $100–300
Chair booster seat $60

Car seats
Convertible $300–500
Forward facing $170–250
Booster seat $90
Extension straps

Safety aids
Baby monitor $70–200
Outlet plugs $4
Cupboard latches $4
Fridge latch $7
Stove guard $8
Taps guard $10
VCR lock $9
Corner cushions $4
Slip-resistant bath mat $9
Baby-on-board sign $5
Door barrier $40–60
Stairway gate $80–140

WHAT DON'T YOU NEED?

Knowing how to save money is partly about knowing what you don't need. Not easy for a first-time parent faced with a bewildering array of products. The following suggestions can help.

Avoid unnecessary items

Some items simply aren't necessary. You can do without them altogether or you can improvise.

Change tables fit into this category. How about just buying a padded change mat and changing your baby on the floor? Not on a bed, of course, due to the risk that your child might roll off. But a mat on the floor is simple and cheap, there's no risk of your baby falling, and you don't need to waste valuable space. It can save you around $50 to $200. This may not be practical for everyone, however. If you have back problems that make it difficult for you to get down on the floor you might appreciate the convenience of a change table. If you are unsure, and think getting down on the floor might cause future back problems, it's worth forking out the extra after all. Remember that the useful lifespan of a change table is quite limited. Even though your child might be in nappies for two to three years, you might find changing a strong and wriggling toddler rather challenging at that height.

Another example of an item that may not be necessary is a nappy bin. There are types on the market that claim to store nappies hygienically and without odour. They can be convenient, but surely it's not too hard to wrap the nappy in a plastic bag and throw it in your outdoor bin? (Harder for people in high rise units, granted.) Forgoing this item will save you $50 or thereabouts. Or you might decide to be even more money conscious and go for cloth nappies.

Avoid doubling up

Often you are presented with a choice. Buy two items that each fulfil a separate purpose, or buy one item that satisfies both.

When deciding, check the price. Usually it's cheaper to buy the single adaptable item, but don't assume this is necessarily so.

An example of doubling up is buying both a pram and a stroller. Prams allow the baby to lay flat, while strollers sit them upright. It's possible to buy a product that converts by the use of a reclining back. Generally once babies reach about six months, they try to crane themselves up so that they can see what is going on around them.

Another area where you may be doubling up is cots and bassinettes. The latter refers to those pretty upraised baskets used for very young babies. A bassinette's lifespan is particularly short—basically only a few months. Consider placing your baby straight into a cot, following the instructions for the prevention of SIDS (see http://www.sidsaustralia.org.au).

Avoid unsafe items

Some items have a dubious safety history and are worth avoiding purely on that basis. That you also save money by doing so is a bonus.

Baby walkers and jumpers are the first things that spring to mind. There have been many calls to have baby walkers banned from sale in Australia, none yet successful. The problem with baby walkers is that they can fall downstairs or tip over. Even a slight change in the surface level can unbalance them. They also make babies effectively taller and more mobile, so they can reach an entire new level of hazards, including irons, boiling pots and your coffee mug.

Osteopaths and chiropractors advise against jumpers because unequal weight can be placed on baby's hips and spine, leading to later problems.

Bodies such as Kidsafe and the Australian Consumers' Association suggest that you find other ways to keep your baby amused. You'll save in the region of $100–200, but most importantly you may be saving your baby from serious injury.

Consider secondhand if safe

You might have friends or family with older children, or you might find a bargain at a garage sale or secondhand store. Perhaps you have made contacts at daycare/preschool/school where you can buy or borrow used equipment.

Secondhand and hand-me-down items can save you a considerable amount of money, but are only worth considering if they don't create a safety hazard. As always, exercise judgement.

For example, older cots do not necessarily conform to modern safety standards and can pose a significant risk. Before accepting an offer for a hand-me-down cot, do all the necessary research and ensure the cot complies. If there is any uncertainty turn it down, even at the risk of offending the well-meaning giver.

The same goes for prams and high chairs. Antique prams and high chairs can be charming, but first check that they're not dangerous.

There are some areas where you can happily accept hand-me-downs: clothes, books, cot sheets, blankets and towels. Maybe just add the proviso that it is best to choose clothes, especially nighties and pyjamas, which have a reduced risk of catching fire. Check labels if they are still attached and not faded.

When it comes to toys be more careful. Old toys might be weakened and have parts that could break off to form a choking hazard. They might be painted with lead paint if they are particularly old.

Consider hiring

Have you considered hiring equipment? It can be a good way to save money on items that you will only need for a short time.

It's possible to hire car seats and/or baby capsules, but you need to be very careful. Straps can become worn from over use and from exposure to the sun. It is much safer to buy a new one. While you're at it, make sure you have it fitted by a professional. The store can advise you of the availability of restraint fitting stations, or you can call your state's traffic authority.

If you end up breastfeeding you can hire one item with confidence, however. An electric breast pump. You can buy manual or battery powered ones at a relatively modest cost, but the electric ones are the fastest and easiest to use and also the most expensive to buy. Mini electric pumps can cost around $200. Standard sized ones cost considerably more.

Electric breast pumps can be hired from some pharmacies or from the Australian Breastfeeding Association (formerly known as the Nursing Mother's Association of Australia). The Association hires pumps for around $20 per week, and members receive a discount. You need to purchase your own milk collection kit; prices depend on the type of pump hired.

Gifts from family and friends

People are going to ask you what you need for your baby. Don't become all coy and vague. Tell them what you want. They're going to buy something anyway. It may as well be something useful.

Sharing with other families

We're always telling children to share, even though we as adults rarely do. Not outside our own families, anyway. But sharing may well be a good way to cut down on the costs associated with young children. If you have close friends who are having a baby around the same time as you, it may be worth asking them to go halves in some expenses and share the equipment.

Obviously this won't work for essential, everyday items. Rather it will be for things you need only occasionally. Think travelling with a baby. You won't be doing this every day. Even if you do it only once, you may still need to buy basic equipment. If you and your friends can coordinate your travel plans so that they don't overlap, you can save by sharing.

The travel cot is an obvious starting point. Many hotels have cots, but there's no guaranteeing their condition and you are usually charged an extra fee anyway. Many parents feel better using their own fold-up travel cot that they know has satisfied safety requirements.

Jogger strollers (those large three-wheeled strollers that look like they could fit a whole family) can also be useful on holiday, particularly if you want to do a lot of roughish walking. Pricey compared to normal strollers, but not so bad if the costs are shared. There are also smaller, more 'citified' versions of the jogger strollers, costing less than the large ones. For travelling that does not involve too much rough walking, it may be most convenient to get a lightweight, one-handed-collapse stroller that takes up less space.

Needless to say if you decide to try the sharing option you have to set the ground rules from the outset. Work out where the product will reside when not in use, and who gets it when. Maybe even jot your agreement down in writing to avoid future misunderstandings. Sharing can save you money—just make sure it doesn't end up costing you a friend.

COSTS OF IMPROVING THE SAFETY OF YOUR HOME

We've already examined the need to consider safety when buying any product for your child, be it pram, cot, high chair etc. Here we are talking about the need to purchase safety aids—or products whose sole function is to help reduce the risk of death and injury. Notice I said *help* reduce the risk. It's not possible to completely eliminate every single source of danger. Nothing can be a substitute for adequate adult supervision.

Reducing risk is an essential part of preparing for a baby, but often overlooked in the first few months of the baby's life. Although a newborn is not able to crawl to power outlets or twist taps, it isn't long before they develop these strange new powers. It's all too easy to be surprised by the rate at which they develop. One moment they can't roll, the next moment they can. You really do need to tackle safety issues right from the outset—preferably before the baby arrives, as you'll be rather busy afterwards. If money constraints prevent that, then as soon as possible after the birth.

This is one area where it certainly doesn't pay to skimp.

Accessories

There are many products you can buy to make your home safer. They are available from department stores, baby specialist stores, and some supermarkets. As you will see, most are remarkably inexpensive. Do some further research to find the particular products that best suit your needs. And always make sure you follow the manufacturer's instructions as to installation, usage and maintenance.

Baby monitor

This is one of the few costly items. Baby monitors retail at about $70 to $200, depending on the style and features. You place the transmitter in the baby's room while the receiver stays with you, allowing you to hear if he or she wakes and cries. Some are noise activated and others continually transmit background noise. Monitors free you to do other things around the house while your baby is sleeping.

Outlet plugs

For some reason babies and toddlers are attracted to the most dangerous things in the house. It's as if some force is beckoning them. And at floor level, power outlets are a tragedy waiting to happen. There are various types of outlet plugs on the market. Some have a little key that you use to remove the plug, others a panel to press. Others you just need to prise out and hope your fingernails are up to the challenge. A packet of twelve plugs will only set you back a few dollars.

Cupboard latches

This is partly for your sanity as well as for safety. Little children love opening cupboard doors and drawers and rifling through the contents. Replacing tea towels every ten minutes can become tiring.

Latches can be fitted to both cupboard doors and drawers. Very young children do not have the dexterity to operate them. For adults, the longer ones are easier to use than the shorter cheaper ones. You might want to allow access to some cupboards, however, to stop your child wrestling with the rest. Place some toys or safe utensils (such as plastic bowls) in a kitchen cupboard to help keep junior amused while you cook.

When it comes to storing particularly dangerous items, don't just rely on latches. They can be broken if the door is yanked forcefully enough. Medicines and chemicals should be stored in cupboards out of children's reach, with an elbow latch (a lock making it physically impossible for a child to open the cupboard if attached according to instructions).

Fridge latch

Stops kids opening the fridge and, as often happens, leaving it open. They retail for under $10.

Stove guard and stove knob covers

Can help prevent burns and accidents with gas by stopping children twisting gas knobs. There are also types that help prevent children opening oven and microwave doors. Generally under $10.

Tap guard

Many children have been burnt by turning on hot water taps. Placing guards on taps can help prevent this. Tap guards are around the $10 mark. It's also worth turning down your water heater's operating temperature to stop the water getting too hot in the first place.

VCR lock

How many people have discovered pieces of toast in their VCR? If you can't keep your VCR out of reach, you can at least insert a lock that prevents items being inserted into the video slot. Again, expect to pay around the $10 mark.

Corner cushions

Sharp edges on tables and other items of furniture can deliver a nasty knock to delicate heads. Corner cushions attach onto the sharp edges and provide a softer, flatter surface. They only cost a few dollars.

Slip resistant bath mat

These come into their own once you pass the baby bath stage. Some take the form of little shaped panels that you place at regular intervals; others are a single large mat that sticks by suction. They never replace the need for adult supervision, of course. Bath mats are around the $10 mark.

Baby on board sign

These warn other drivers to be aware that the driver of this car might not be as focused as they ought to be. Babies crying and children quarrelling can be a distraction to even the best driver.

Door barrier

You may have some rooms or sections of rooms that you would like to keep out of bounds. Generally consisting of two panels with bars, door barriers can be stretched across the doorway and fastened into place. Make sure they are on securely and that you cannot push them over. They cost approximately $40–60.

Stairway gate

Stairs pose one of the greatest hazards in the home. You can purchase gates that can only be opened and closed by adults—young children have neither the strength nor dexterity to operate the opening mechanism. Consider placing one at the top and one at the bottom of the stairs, wherever the child has access. Stairway gates start at around $80 but are worth every cent.

Permanent changes to your home

The above accessories are used for the first few years of your child's life, and then gradually the need for them diminishes. There may need to be some changes, however, that are permanent.

Safety cut off switch

This works by cutting off the power supply in a fraction of a second, drastically reducing the risk of electrocution. Different types exist to suit varying needs. Call an electrician for advice and installation.

Security doors

They keep intruders out and wandering toddlers in.

Pool fences

So obvious they're hardly worth mentioning, but I will anyway. Apart from legal requirements, pool fences are essential for any thoughtful homeowner. Even if your children are older and know how to swim, you still need to protect potential visitors.

And don't forget the need to protect any 'uninvited' visitors—neighbourhood children who might wander onto your property when you don't expect it.

A less obvious danger is posed by wading pools. Young children can drown in only a few inches of water. Once the (supervised) wading session is over, empty the pool and don't leave it where it can collect rainwater.

Safe appliances

Check general appliances periodically to ensure that they are not wearing out. Check that electrical cords are not frayed, that switches operate safely, and that handles/straps are not worn.

Safe heating system

We tend to re-use home heating appliances and water heaters year in and out without giving much thought as to whether they are still in good working order. Take some time to ensure that there are no gas leaks or other potential faults.

Safe environment

Give your home the quick once over. Do you have worn carpets that could cause people to trip? Broken tiles? Slippery floors? Does your home need re-wiring? Fixing these items may be costly, but will need to be tackled at some stage before the problem worsens.

FURTHER HELP

- The Australian Consumers' Association has reports on baby products and safety that can be viewed online. You can either purchase a membership that includes those reports or purchase the ability to view a single report as often as you like for a set period. See http://www.choice.com.au.
- The Child Accident Prevention Foundation of Australia (Kidsafe) is an independent organisation dedicated to the prevention of death and injury of children. See their website at http://www.kidsafe.com.au for safety fact sheets.

- The Ministerial Council on Consumer Affairs has released a nursery furniture guide, available through your state's consumer affairs/fair trading department, publications section. Also see http://www.consumer.gov.au.

Useful books and publications

Ministerial Council on Consumer Affairs 1998, 'Keeping baby safe: A guide to nursery furniture'

Australian Consumers' Association 2003, *The Choice Guide to Baby Products*, 8th edn, Choice Books, Sydney.

Clegg, M. 2003, *Your Baby on a Budget*, New Holland Publishers, Sydney.

5

The family budget

A budget sounds like a lot of fuss. And it is. But it's worth it.

Budgets are the best way to take control of your finances. Just the mere act of creating one allows you to see where you overspend, where you can make cuts, and how much you are able to save.

Many people are put off by the idea of a budget. You may have heard them say something like, 'They're too restricting. I want to enjoy my money and a budget won't let me.'

On the contrary, budgets are liberating.

Often when you buy yourself a luxury, there's a niggling doubt deep down that you really can't afford it. You buy it anyway, but like a dieter sneaking chocolate you don't feel quite right. If you have a budget, you know exactly what you can and can't afford. Factor in spending on luxuries, and you know what you can buy, and when. And if there's something you want to get that temporarily blows out your budget, you can adjust your spending later to balance it out again.

A budget is not meant to be set in concrete. It evolves, adjusts and exists to serve you.

So when should you make one? Before you have children or after? When they're babies or when they're big? The answer is—right now. Or next time you have a few free hours on your hands. Your budget will change anyway, regardless of when you make it. If you don't have children yet, create your budget with an eye to saving up to start your family. If you do, then create it with the aim of keeping costs under control and saving for the future. The basic goal of any budget is always the same: to improve your financial position. The reason why you need one varies with your ambitions and your life stage.

Creating a budget is not difficult, but it is time consuming. This chapter provides step-by-step instructions for the creation of your own family budget. The worksheets make the task easier.

But there's more to it than just making the budget. This chapter also looks at how to use your budget. It's not a matter of slavishly sticking to predetermined figures. Rather it's a question of keeping track, making ongoing adjustments, and building in balance.

CREATING YOUR OWN BUDGET

The process is really quite simple. All you need is a pen and paper, a few spare hours, and perhaps a glass of wine for courage. Dig out your bills, receipts, invoices, tax records, and any other documents that relate to your finances. Photocopy the following worksheets then follow the four steps below. If you prefer to use a computer, you can enter the categories on a spreadsheet program, which will do the adding up for you.

Step 1: Income

The first step is possibly the quickest and easiest. List your income from all the varied sources on the first worksheet (Worksheet 5.1). Be careful not to overlook anything. Typical sources include the obvious wage/salary, as well as interest, rent, dividends, government benefits. There may be more, for example, trust distributions.

We're looking at your disposable income, by the way. Tax payments and compulsory superannuation contributions made by your employer on your behalf have been subtracted on this worksheet. Additional voluntary contributions are an investment, which will come out of surplus income. But more on that later.

If you currently have a partner and you want to create a family budget, make sure you include his or her income too.

You may find it easiest to write down how much you earn in an entire year, particularly if your income fluctuates. This also helps you take account of infrequent incomings such as tax returns, bonuses and royalties. Divide the total annual figure by twelve to arrive at a monthly sum. Just keep in mind that the actual amount you have in some months might be higher or lower than the figure you arrived at.

If you prefer to follow a weekly budget, simply divide all your figures by 52. It doesn't matter, as long as you are consistent.

Worksheet 5.1: Estimating your income

Enter yearly figures then adjust for a monthly result.

Earnings

Salary/wage (gross)	$__________________
Overtime payments	$__________________
Bonuses	$__________________
Commissions	$__________________
Other	$__________________

Investment income

Interest	$__________________
Rent	$__________________
Dividends	$__________________
Trust distribution	$__________________
Other	$__________________

Other sources

Government allowances	$__________________
Tax refund	$__________________
Child support/spousal maintenance	$__________________
Other	$__________________

TOTAL ANNUAL INCOME	$__________________
Minus compulsory superannuation	$__________________
Minus taxation	$__________________
Equals DISPOSABLE INCOME	$__________________

Divide by 12 to arrive at

MONTHLY DISPOSABLE INCOME $__________________

Step 2: Estimated outgoings

Now we start getting more fidgety. Because there are so many expenses that we encounter it's easy to overlook a particular item, so you need to give the issue a great deal of thought.

But there's something else to keep in mind. Here we have, to some degree, an element of choice. Not many of us have the ability to control our income, but we do have the power to control certain aspects of our spending. You'll see that the outgoings worksheet (Worksheet 5.2) is divided into two major sections—fixed expenses and variable expenses.

As you start to fill in the relevant spaces, you will realise that something very important is happening. Without even completing your budget, you are starting to identify areas where you may be overspending and where you have the ability to cut back. Sometimes you have no choice—rent is rent, after all, and apart from tackling the landlord or moving house you have little control. But you do have the ability to cut back on other types of expenses: the amount you spend on takeaway meals, for instance.

Sometimes there are overlaps between fixed and variable expenses, but for the sake of simplicity, these are not reflected in the worksheet. Telephone costs, for instance, are listed as fixed expenses, as much of the cost relates to line and handset rental. But the amount of calls you make varies and is controllable. There's no point being too pedantic, however. Just keep in mind that some fixed expenses are more fixed than others are.

We also come into some practical difficulties. Most of us have written records of how much we earn, but not how much we spend. You probably keep bills, at least for a while, but what about shopping receipts? Maybe for the big items that might need to be returned, but not for the odd coffee or ice cream here and there, or all those trivial trinkets kids keep asking for. But these seemingly insignificant expenses add up. Slowly but surely.

You might find that you cannot fill in all the spaces in one sitting. You might need to start paying attention to your spending habits over the next few weeks. Keep records to get an idea of the general patterns. It's a bit like a dieter listing all they eat in a day. Like overeating, overspending is insidious. It may be hard to notice until you actually put it all down on paper and add it up.

There's something else.

In Step 1 we looked at yearly figures and divided down for a monthly result. It's hard to say how much you spend on groceries in a year. But if you only look at a monthly timeframe you might overlook less frequent expenses such as bills and insurance premiums. To overcome this problem we've used a monthly timeframe but included irregular and infrequent expenses. When you fill in the spaces, keep in mind that you need to adjust. Divide quarterly bills by three, yearly expenses by twelve and so forth.

Worksheet 5.2: Estimating your expenses

Calculated on a monthly basis. Adjust timeframe for less frequent expenditures.

Fixed expenses
Housing
Rent or board $__________________________
Council rates $__________________________
Gas $__________________________
Electricity $__________________________
Water rates $__________________________
Telephone (inc. mobile) $__________________________
Maintenance and repairs $__________________________

Transport
Car registration $__________________________
Petrol $__________________________
Maintenance and repairs $__________________________
Parking fees $__________________________
Licence $__________________________
Motor vehicle association fee $__________________________
Public transport $__________________________
Taxis $__________________________

Insurance
Home building $__________________________
Home contents $__________________________

Motor vehicle $________________________________
Life, trauma $________________________________
Private health $________________________________
Income protection insurance $________________________________

Interest payments
Home loan repayment $________________________________
Car loan repayments $________________________________
Personal loans $________________________________
Investment loans $________________________________

Family
Childcare $________________________________
School/education fees $________________________________
School uniforms, shoes etc. $________________________________
Text books, stationery etc. $________________________________
Other school costs (e.g. excursions) $________________________________
Child support/spousal maintenance $________________________________

Other
Other fixed expenses $________________________________

Variable expenses
Shopping
Groceries (inc. food) $________________________________
Takeaway meals $________________________________
Alcohol $________________________________
Clothing and shoes $________________________________
Fashion accessories $________________________________
Cosmetics $________________________________
Hair and skin care $________________________________

Medical/health
Doctor $________________________________
Dentist $________________________________
Optometrist $________________________________
Chemist $________________________________
Other (e.g. alternative therapies) $________________________________
Gym membership $________________________________

Entertainment/leisure
Restaurants/bars/cafes $________________________________
Concerts/theatre $________________________________

Movies/videos $______________________

Pay TV subscription $______________________

Internet subscription $______________________

Magazines/newspapers $______________________

CDs, books, software $______________________

Holidays $______________________

Hobbies, extracurricular activities $______________________

Services

Hairdressers $______________________

Beauticians $______________________

Dry cleaning $______________________

Gardeners $______________________

Home help $______________________

Nannies/babysitters $______________________

Other

Home improvements $______________________

Gardening supplies $______________________

Furniture/appliances $______________________

Gifts $______________________

Credit card repayments $______________________

Contributions to charity $______________________

Other $______________________

TOTAL MONTHLY EXPENSES $______________________

Step 3: Compare and consider

Now is the time of reckoning. The third step requires you to compare the results of Steps 1 and 2. Go back to your worksheets and compare the totals. Subtract your total monthly outgoings from your monthly disposable income and listen for the drum roll.

So what's the result? Are you in surplus or deficit? By how much?

If you're in deficit

If you are in deficit or only just breaking even, you need to take a hard look at your expenses. Focus most of your attention on the variable costs, but remember that there may still be scope to cut back on fixed costs. As mentioned before, some are more fixed than others. Try reducing your phone bill by making fewer calls, saving electricity by switching off lights and appliances when not in use, and cutting down on petrol costs by walking more and driving less.

But it's in the area of variable costs where you'll find the greatest potential to save. Can you spend less on luxuries and leisure activities? If you're in the habit of buying a takeaway meal once a week, could you cut that down to once a fortnight? That in itself could save you around $40 to $50 per month. What about pay TV, magazine subscriptions and club memberships? Do you really need them, or is there some leeway there? Can you put off plans for renovations and home decorating for the moment?

You might need to look more closely at other items, such as grocery shopping. Say you normally spend $200 a week on food and groceries. Can you cut it down to $180? It may require you to be more alert to prices and specials, and to cut back on impulse buys. You know the rules. Don't go shopping on an empty stomach. Make a shopping list and use it, avoiding the temptation to buy things you don't really need. Small trivial items add up rapidly, and you can cut them back without any great trauma.

If you are currently pregnant or trying to be, you'll find some expenses will naturally fall—for instance, money previously spent on alcohol and/or cigarettes. Restaurants lose much of their appeal to those suffering from morning sickness. Although the aim is not necessarily to save money, the outcome nevertheless helps you with your budget.

Other savings may require rather more thought. Throughout this book you will find money saving suggestions that can help.

But say you've already cut back right to the bone, and can't find any areas where you can easily cut back further. Then what? Hopefully there's a way to increase your income. Ask for a raise, get a better job, look at government assistance if applicable, or try turning a hobby into a money earning activity. Or maybe there's something you can sell to help ease the pressure.

Let's get pessimistic now and assume you can't boost your income, at least in the short-term. There may still be some steps to take—but keep in mind that these are not sensible long-term strategies. They are only for temporary use when other avenues fail, and once your situation improves, these measures should be discarded. Does that sound ominous enough? Good.

So, when desperate, you can consider:

- cutting your home loan repayments back to the minimum;
- reducing your voluntary super contributions;
- cutting your private health insurance down to the most basic cover; or
- drawing on your past savings or reduce any current savings.

It's also wise to seek professional help, particularly if you are having problems meeting your debts.

What to do with your surplus

Maybe you are in the happy situation where you are actually in surplus. If so, what should you do with it?

Clearly you should be saving some of your excess funds. How much you save depends on many things: the size of the surplus; your goals; your timeframe for meeting those goals; and whether you want to enjoy some of that surplus right now in the form of a few extra luxuries. It's fine to spend some of your money on items that are not strictly necessary. As long as you know how much you can afford, you can factor some more spending into your budget.

But the important thing is to work out a savings strategy. A good approach is to decide how much you want to save per month and write this down on your expenses worksheet. Place it under fixed expenses, to reinforce the message that this is an essential and regular part of your future spending habits.

The amount you save might be for a specific purpose—for instance to start a family. But once that purpose is satisfied, it's still important to keep up some sort of savings program. Figures may change as your needs and circumstances change, but the important thing is to keep on saving.

Once your savings start to grow you may want to consider

ways to make your money work harder. Chapter 13, 'Securing your children's financial future' considers the various choices you have when it comes to investing your money.

Step 4: Create

Time to actually make your budget. Go back to your estimated expenses worksheet. On a fresh blank copy, write how much you would like to be spending on each category. Some, particularly the fixed costs, will be the same as in your original calculation. Others will reflect cuts you feel you ought to make. For instance, if you were previously spending $100 per month on café lunches, you might want to try cutting that down to $80 per month. Don't forget that for expenses that arise less frequently than monthly (such as quarterly bills) you are actually entering how much you need to set aside each month to meet those expenses when they arise.

And, most importantly, don't forget to add a savings category.

If you found you were in a comfortable surplus, you may want to factor in spending on the odd luxury. It's also a good idea to build in some slack so that if unexpected expenses arise, there's room to meet them. You can do this in two ways—by keeping some over each time, and/or by being flexible in the way you use your budget.

Check that the total, including savings, equals your total disposable income as per the first worksheet.

That's it. There's your budget. Not so hard after all.

USING YOUR BUDGET

Creating your budget is one thing—actually using it is another. Some people start all fired up with enthusiasm, only to have that enthusiasm wane after a few months. The reason isn't boredom. Often it's because of the way they use their budget.

For some, a budget is something to be slavishly adhered to, where everything is regulated down to the last cent. Spend $x on toothpaste and $y on soap. Almost a form of punishment.

But that's not how it should be. A budget should be something to make life easier, not harder. It's there to guide and assist, not dictate.

So how should you use it?

You don't need to take the budget with you when you go shopping. Rather, try to keep your limits in mind. This is simple when purchasing clothes, shoes and so forth. But it's not so easy when grocery shopping, as it's hard to mentally add up all the purchases as you go. Just do your best to keep costs low and see how things go. In other words, keep track.

Keeping track

Bills are often not what you expected. Charges can rise, even if your usage doesn't. Make a note of how much you are paying out.

Similarly, keep receipts from shopping and other outgoings. Once a month or so sift through them to see if you are indeed spending as much as you intended.

If you overspent slightly on one item while simultaneously underspending on another, that's fine. As long as you have overall balance. If one month you blow your budget, make up for it the next month.

If, however, you find you are consistently going over or under budget, you may need to make a few adjustments.

Making adjustments

From time to time you may need to adjust your budget. Initially you created it based on your estimated expenditures. As you begin to use it you may find these estimates don't match with what you are actually spending, so some fine tuning may be required.

Your life circumstances may also change. Getting a new job, having a baby, leaving the workforce for a while when you have that baby—all these things will require changes to your budget. But don't worry. Once you've prepared your initial budget, you'll find making adjustments relatively quick and easy.

FURTHER HELP

- For tips on creating budgets, visit the website of the Credit Union Services Corporation (CUSCAL), the credit union's representative body, at http://www.cuscal.com.au. The Australian Securities and Investments Commission's consumer website is also very helpful—see http://www.fido.asic.gov.au. Many private companies in the finance industry also have budget tips on their websites.

Useful publications

Credit Union Services Corporation (CUSCAL) 1997, 'Budgeting: Making it easy',
James, V. 2003, *The Woman's Money Book*, revised edn, Allen & Unwin, Sydney.

Part 2

The early years

6

Ongoing costs

So you thought *preparing* for a baby was expensive. That was only the beginning. There are many ongoing costs to contend with after your baby has arrived. Food. Clothing. Toys. Entertainment. All important, and all potentially pricey.

Recently NATSEM (the National Centre for Social Economic Modelling) published a report examining the costs involved in raising a family. Sponsored by AMP, the *AMP-NATSEM Income and Wealth Report*, Issue 3, October 2002 is unsettlingly titled 'All they need is love . . . and around $450 000'. It can be downloaded from the AMP website at http://www.amp.com.au. The title derives from a finding that it costs approximately $448 000 for the average family to raise two children from birth to age 20. This equates to $310 per week. Ouch.

But don't panic.

In coming to this figure they created a hypothetical family in an attempt to represent the typical Australian family. Of course you may not follow the same patterns and the figures may not represent your situation at all. Some families spend hundreds a week; others get by with far less. How do they do it? The tips in this and other chapters will show you how.

The following table appears in the report and looks at how much people *might* be spending per week on their children. It is reproduced with the kind permission of AMP and NATSEM.

Table 6.1: Estimated expenditure by category, by age of child, March 2002

Expenditure category	0–4	5–9	10–14	15–17	18–24
Housing	$45	$25	$9	$14	–$9
Transport	–$3	$35	$40	$65	$95
Recreation	–$3	$23	$40	$41	$54
Education and childcare	$25	$23	$23	$37	$27
Food	$12	$41	$46	$58	$68
Clothing	$11	$12	$6	$23	$18
Other	$14	$5	$45	$79	$69
TOTAL	$102	$164	$209	$318	$322

Source: AMP-NATSEM Income and Wealth Report, Issue 3, October 2002

You may have noticed some of the figures are negatives, meaning families are spending less than childless couples who are at the same living standard. It's not too hard to guess why people with very young children spend less on transport and recreation than childless couples.

Naturally some of these costs (housing, for instance) would arise even if you didn't have children, but if you have a family your needs are different (a larger house, for example). Housing costs are highest with respect to young children because most families buy their home early on, the mortgage falling as the children grow. Most costs, however, increase as children grow.

But there is some good news. The report also found that the costs of second and subsequent children fall. Many items can be re-used by later children, such as baby equipment, clothing, toys and books.

There are many items listed on the table where savings can be made. Recreation, food, equipment and other costs can all be trimmed without detriment. Having a budget (discussed in the previous chapter) is the first step towards taking control of your ongoing expenses.

The next step involves knowing where you can cut back without compromising your child's wellbeing. And that's the subject of this chapter.

NAPPIES

The debate between cloth and disposable nappies has been raging for 30-something years, since disposables first appeared on the scene. Clearly disposables cost more, but exactly how much more? You might decide that the convenience justifies the strain on your wallet, but just be sure you know what you're letting yourself in for.

Cloth

Cloth nappies are indisputably cheaper. You will need to buy two to three packets at the outset, each containing a dozen nappies. This will cost you around $60 to $90. They may last until toilet training time, or you might find you need another packet or two. You will also need some plastic pants to pull over the top (a few dollars per multi-pack) and nappy pins or the equivalent (also only a few dollars). You can buy nappy liners to help keep your baby dryer, but they are not essential. A decent-sized nappy bucket will set you back about $10 to $15. After that, your only outlays are for detergents and the water and energy costs of doing the laundry.

Some people baulk at the extra work involved in washing, drying and folding nappies. But others find that once they get into the swing of things, it all just becomes part of the routine.

Cloth nappies are also far more environmentally friendly, and can be re-enlisted as dusting rags when your child is finally past the nappy stage.

The thought of lugging wet and dirty nappies around on outings is unpleasant, however, and it's possible to compromise. Many parents use cloth nappies at home and disposables when they go out.

Disposables

If you use disposable nappies only, expect to pay about $15 to $30 a week. The actual amount depends on which brand you use, where you do your shopping, and the age of your child.

There are various brands available on the market, some cheaper than others. The cheaper ones may not necessarily be better value, however, as they may need to be changed more frequently. If you decide to use disposables, do your own trial comparisons before settling down to one brand. Even then, look out for decent products that are on special. It's also a good idea to ask other parents which products they use and why.

Buying in bulk can be a good way to save, but don't assume. Check the prices before you automatically go for the bumper size box. And only buy in bulk if you're confident your baby won't outgrow that size before the product is used up. Not likely to be a problem for disposables-only babies, but if you restrict your usage to major outings only, you may find you have too many on your hands.

Nappy service

This is a service that regularly provides you with clean cloth nappies. Dirty nappies are taken away (usually weekly) and replaced with clean ones. You have the environmental advantages of cloth without the extra work. You do lose the cost-saving advantage, however. Nappy service prices vary and you need to shop around, but, generally speaking, they are not much cheaper than buying disposables.

Wipes and lotions

You will also need to add a small regular sum for botty wipes and lotions. Or, if you prefer, simply use a dampened face washer, which you then toss in the nappy bucket. When it comes to toiletries, soap-free bath lotion and baby shampoo are a good basis. If you need nappy rash treatment, seek advice from the baby clinic, your GP or a chemist.

BREAST OR BOTTLE?

The choice between breast and bottle feeding is very much a lifestyle issue. Your attitudes and parenting decisions come into play far more than financial issues. Do keep in mind, however, that your decision will have a significant impact on your ongoing daily costs.

Formula

Depending on the age of your baby and whether solids have been introduced, you can expect to pay around $15 to $30 per week for formula. Add the costs of bottles (say $5–10 each but this varies markedly between brands) and the costs of sterilisation.

You can sterilise baby bottles by chemical or heat methods. Chemical sterilisers cost around $20 for the unit and a few dollars for the solution. You can buy relatively inexpensive heat sterilisers that you pop into the microwave oven. At around the $50 to $60 mark they are cheaper than the plug-in equivalents, but generally hold fewer bottles. Plug-in models will set you back around $150. The cheapest way to sterilise bottles is to stick them into a big pot of boiling water.

Breastfeeding

What can I say? Breastfeeding is free. It's also convenient, easy (once you get the hang of it), portable, has health benefits for the baby and aids bonding. Of course not everyone who wants to breastfeed is actually able to. If you are having difficulty breastfeeding and you decide that's what you want to do, seek the advice of your doctor and/or a lactation consultant.

Breast pumps give you the ability to express your milk into a bottle for times when you can't be there to feed your baby personally. Manual ones are fairly inexpensive, say $40 to $100, but take some getting used to. Electric ones can be hired from some pharmacists or from the Australian Breastfeeding Association for around $20 per week. You need to buy your own milk collection kits but they are fairly inexpensive. Or you can buy a mini electric breast pump for around $200. A lactation expert can help you decide which sort best meets your needs.

FEEDING YOUR BABY

Few things are more eagerly awaited than giving that first spoonful of 'real' food. The astonished look on that little face is relished by every parent. Quite a world away from the teenager who inhales the contents of your fridge. Although babies only eat small amounts, there's still scope to save on the costs of meals.

Commercially prepared baby food is convenient and a good idea for outings, but if used as the sole source it can be quite expensive. The amount you would spend depends on the age and appetite of your child, as well as the brands you purchase, but $15 to $25 a week would not be an unrealistic figure for an older baby.

By preparing your own baby food you can save a considerable sum: you only pay for the costs of the ingredients. For the sake of convenience try making a large batch and freezing the meals in single portions, starting with ice-cube trays then moving to jars as baby grows. It's a good idea to clean and keep empty jars.

It all adds up

Hannah's case is a rather extreme one, but serves well as an illustration.

Hannah bottle fed her baby from birth to age twelve months. The cost of formula fluctuated as her baby grew and started eating solids. All together she spent $960 on formula.

She also used disposable nappies. Again, the cost varied as her child grew. Hannah found toilet training much harder than expected, and baby Jonathon ended up wearing nappies for nearly three-and-a-half years. Overall Hannah spent $3215 on nappies and wipes.

She only used commercially prepared food for Jonathon from age four to twelve months. He ate little in the first two of those months, and then suddenly his appetite took off. Hannah spent $370 on prepared food.

She could have breastfed Jonathon for twelve months at zero cost, putting him straight onto cow's milk at the end of his first year. She could have used cloth nappies primarily and saved disposables for major outings only—say this would have cost her under $900 over the entire nappy period of three-and-a-half years. She could have made most of Jonathon's food herself and only used prepared food for outings—say at a cost of under $100 over the first twelve months.

All up Hannah spent $4545 on these everyday baby costs when she quite reasonably could have got away with under $1000.

CLOTHING AND FOOTWEAR

The considerations aren't that different to buying these items for yourself. You can buy a shirt for a few dollars or a few hundred. It all depends on your tastes and budget.

There is one major difference, of course. Children grow rapidly, especially in the first two years. Don't buy too much in one size. If buying in advance make sure you are buying the right season's clothes to match the time your baby will be the right size to wear them. (Frustratingly, this is an issue that gift givers often overlook.)

This leads to the question—what size should you buy? All babies are different and grow at different rates so it is impossible to be definitive. As a general guide, however, size 0000 is for the tiniest newborn and unless your baby is premature, may not be worth buying. Sizes 000 to 00 may take them to six months, by which time they could be wearing size 0. After that, just follow the numbers. A one-year-old might wear a size 1, a two-year-old a size 2, and so on, pretty much until they hit adult sizes. Not all children fit this pattern so try clothes on your child wherever possible.

So what will you need? As a starting point, consider purchasing:

- four to six singlets—size 000 or 00—about $3 each;
- four to six nighties or all-in-one romper outfits—size 00 or 000—about $10 each;
- a few pairs of socks or booties (shoes aren't necessary until baby starts to walk)—about $3–4 each;
- a couple of jumpers or cardigans, more for winter babies—about $10 each; and
- a couple of hats to protect them from the sun and/or to prevent heat loss—about $5–10 each.

These prices are averages only and can be higher or lower depending on where you do your shopping and the quality of the items purchased.

Say you decide to buy five singlets, five romper suits, two pairs of booties, two jumpers and two hats. By the above figures it could cost you about $100. Depending on how fast your baby grows, this will only last you for a few months.

When making your purchase, consider the quality of the clothes. Avoid too many designer labels that will be rapidly outgrown, but also eschew the false economies of the real cheapies that fall apart after a few washes.

Don't overlook the savings that can be made from second-hand and hand-me-down items. You might have friends or family with children older than yours who are willing to pass on outgrown clothes. Or you may be able to buy good quality items at charity stores or through daycare/preschool/school networks.

And, as mentioned earlier, family and friends are likely to buy clothes as gifts. Be upfront about asking for what you need. Specify the size and—if your relationship allows—ask them if they mind hanging on to the receipts. Just in case! Some department stores allow exchange without receipts.

Consider health and safety issues. Try to use items that have a reduced fire hazard risk—particularly important for winter attire.

LOW COST LEISURE ACTIVITIES

Having an enjoyable time with your children should not be conditional on having a bulging wallet. While many leisure activities cost money, there are plenty of ways to have fun without breaking the bank. Ultimately they can be more rewarding than high cost alternatives.

What you do with your children depends on their age, of course, as well as their interests and personalities. You might want them to attend classes, such as music, dance, swimming, or other types of sports. For convenience, these are dealt with in the section on extracurricular expenses in Chapter 11, 'Educating your child'. But they can apply equally to younger children.

You might like to consider some of the following low cost options. I've tried to divide the suggestions up according to age, but naturally there is considerable overlap.

Babies, toddlers and preschoolers

- Join or form a mothers' group. The children get to interact, and you have the opportunity to meet people in a similar situation. A good starting point is your baby's early childhood or baby health care centre.
- Join a playgroup. Some are run by churches, others by community groups. You might be required to pay a small membership fee and/or contribute morning tea occasionally.
- Read to your child. This has educational benefits as well as being enjoyable.
- Make the most of your child's imagination. Young children have fertile imaginations and can often come up with their own ideas to entertain themselves. Do they want to play dress-ups, let's pretend, or make up a story? Don't be afraid to let them take the lead.

Preschoolers and older children

- Videos and movies. Videos are an old standby and not bad for a lazy or rainy day. Movies are rather more costly, but many cinemas admit adults to children's movies at children's prices.
- Organised activities. Various ethnic, community and religious groups organise activities for children either free of charge or at a low cost. Activities may include craft days, play groups, social groups, music days and so on.
- Public libraries. Libraries are not just places for borrowing and returning books, which is great free entertainment in its own right. Many also offer activities such as story telling and craft sessions for preschool aged children. They may also have book lovers' clubs for older children.
- Shopping centres often put on free shows for children during school holidays.
- Scan the local paper. There may be something going on in your own neighbourhood. Street fairs, market days, church and school fetes are all enjoyable ways to involve your children in the local community. You might even pick up a few bargains.

All ages

- Enjoy the great outdoors. We're lucky to live in a country with so many beautiful beaches, parks, and reserves. Pack a picnic to further cut down on the costs of kiosk and cafeteria food.
- Visit friends or family. Often children are satisfied with just a change of scene, especially if there are others their own age they can play with.
- Try crafts and hobbies. Do you like woodwork, gardening, painting or cooking? Can you play a musical instrument or dance? Try involving your children in your hobbies or explore new avenues together.
- Investigate the special family membership for zoos, aquariums etc. For example, Taronga Zoo membership for an adult is around $50 per year for unlimited visits.

All in all, spend time, not money. Savour their childhood. Even if you just spend the afternoon kicking a ball around the backyard or doing jigsaw puzzles on the floor, it's doing it together that counts.

TOYS

Buying toys is not just a financial matter. Safety becomes an important issue here and you need to research the matter thoroughly. Standards Australia sets safety standards for toys and you should check that they have been adhered to.

Beware of cheap toys that can break easily with normal play. Also avoid toys that have built-in hazards (for instance, they contain small parts that can break off and be swallowed) as well as toys that are for the wrong age group. What is safe for an older child can be extremely dangerous for a younger child.

Toy libraries are a great resource. Smaller toys can be borrowed for as little as $1 a week; larger toys, including pedal cars or trikes, from about $5. It's good for very young children to be able to try out different toys, especially when they are young enough not to get violently attached to a particular toy.

Why not improvise? There are many ways to create safe toys that cost very little—and in some cases absolutely nothing. For example:

- What toddler can resist whacking a saucepan with a spoon? Create your own kitchen orchestra out of containers, pots and lids. Supervise the play, of course.
- Preschool aged children love making craft out of odds and ends. Collect household waste products such as toilet roll tubes, juice bottles and egg cartons, along with cotton wool, bits of string and ribbons. You can pick up glitter pens and poster paints cheaply at discount stores and keep them on hand. Discount shops and supermarkets have cheap plastic storage boxes, ideal for storing bits and bobs for craft.
- Preschool aged children also enjoy painting and drawing, which isn't expensive. Play dough is another favourite, and it costs very little to make your own.
- Young school aged children enjoy board games and jigsaws (which needn't cost a lot) and sporting equipment (where prices can vary depending on the items).
- Invest in a toy-making book or put your creativity to the test. It doesn't cost a lot to make your own dolls, puppets, jigsaw puzzles and wheel toys.

Again, ultimately it's the time you spend with your child that counts. Buying expensive toys as a substitute for your time and attention is not going to satisfy a child. Some of the best fun is to be had from making toys and working out activities together.

PETS

Should you agree to your child's request for a pet? This is not just a question of cost, here we are talking about a living being. Can you put in the time to adequately meet its needs? Are you prepared for the impact it will have on your home and garden, not to mention your lifestyle? And are you prepared to make a commitment for the next ten to fifteen years (or however long the pet will live)?

But the money issue obviously is important. It is very hard to generalise, but the following can give you an idea of the types of expenses involved. If your animal falls ill or is injured, vet bills can be measured in the hundreds.

- Pedigree dogs can cost from $500 to $1500 (some sought after cross-breeds can cost nearly as much). Set-up costs include kennel/basket (say $50 to $80), collar and lead, feeding bowls, toys, desexing if desired (about $200 to $300) and vaccinations ($70 or more depending on what's needed), and council registration (cheaper if desexed). Upkeep costs include food (say $1 a day for small dogs), annual vaccinations, flea and worming treatments, microchipping, obedience training, grooming ($50 to $100), and boarding ($15 to $25 per day).
- Pedigree cats can cost $500 to $1500, cross-breeds $150 or so. You need a litter tray (about $15), litter (say $10 to $15 per month), and other items that are similar to those for dogs, with the addition of a scratching post. Desexing is generally cheaper for cats. Food can be around 80c to $1 per day.
- Birds vary in price depending on the type of bird. A humble budgie can cost $20 to $40, cockatiels over $50. More exotic birds can cost a great deal more. Add the costs of a cage ($100 or so depending on size), cage accessories and toys. Ongoing costs include food and supplements, mite and lice spray. All up the ongoing costs can reach or exceed $100 per year for a couple of birds.
- Fish prices also vary markedly. Generally cold water fish are cheaper than tropical. Basic goldfish can cost $3 to $6 each. A tiny bowl can cost $20, a small tank about $60. Add the costs of gravel, plants, decorations, water conditioner and food. You also need a filter and light, as well as a heater for tropical fish, all of which add to your power bill.
- Other popular pets include mice, guinea pigs, rabbits and turtles. You need a hutch or other suitable housing. Mice cost a few dollars, rabbits can be around $40 each.

Even so, you don't have to pay the earth for a loving pet. Mongrels cost considerably less than pure breeds. Or maybe you could rescue a dog or cat by buying one from an animal welfare organisation. They cost around $100 to $200, which includes vaccination, microchipping, desexing and so forth. Also, people often give away animals when their own pets have a litter.

Feeding costs might be trimmed by making your own pet food. Just be sure you know how to make balanced meals so the health of your pet does not suffer. Consider cutting costs by using secondhand equipment such as fish tanks, bird cages, mouse houses and pet baskets. And if you're handy, you can save a considerable sum by building a kennel or hutch yourself.

KIDS' BIRTHDAY PARTIES

Do you cringe when it's that time of year again? Kids' birthday parties seem to be getting more expensive all the time. When we were little we basically just ran around and giggled for a couple of hours. Now things are becoming way more sophisticated. Many parents hold parties at special venues, and those that have them at home often feel the need to supplement the day by hiring equipment such as a jumping castle, or hiring entertainers such as clowns, magicians, fairies, even reptile handlers. The options are endless.

But the costs involved also seem endless.

If you choose to go down the special venue route, you could be paying $10 to $20 per child, depending on the venue and what's included in the price. If your child is one of those that invites the whole class, it can get very pricey.

Party venues include play centres, fast food outlets, bowling alleys, swimming centres, skating rinks etc. The per head figure may not be the whole price, however. Birthday cakes are usually not included in the price, and can easily cost $40 to $50 for a small- to medium-sized party cake. Some venues provide lolly bags and balloons, others expect you to.

If you choose to hire an entertainer for your home party, expect to pay $150 to $200 for one to one-and-a-half hours.

Jumping castles can also cost about the $200 mark, depending on the size.

Even if you try for a low key at-home party without all the frills, costs still add up quickly. Generally you need party food and drinks, special plates and napkins, decorations, balloons, party hats and blowers, small presents for games, and perhaps adult snacks for the parents. If you have more than one child, you could be looking at a few hundred dollars a year, even for the most basic parties.

Not to mention all the presents you need to buy for other children. Particularly in the early years, there are many parties to go to. Most people buy a gift worth around $10 to $15 (more if you are a friend of the parent), and if your child gets invited to ten or more parties per year, gifts alone can cost you a couple of hundred dollars all up.

Money saving suggestions

Nobody wants their child to miss out on such basic childhood pleasures. Maybe you could try some of the following suggestions to cut costs without cutting out the fun:

- Consider venues such as parks or beaches.
- Make most of the party food yourself (the old favourites include fairy bread, chocolate crackles, cup cakes, fruit salad), limiting shop bought items.
- Have a go at making the birthday cake yourself.
- Hire a collection of toys from a toy library.
- Include traditional games like musical chairs and blind man's bluff—they cost virtually nothing!
- Try making a piñata out of papier-mâché. A shop bought one can cost $30 to $50, and you still need to fill it. Your child will enjoy making it with you.
- Consider combined parties, either of siblings/cousins or friends who have birthdays close together.
- Maybe have a party every second year, and use the in-between years for a different kind of treat.
- Suggest having only a small number of friends over for a sleepover.

Keeping them happy

Margaret had three children aged three, seven and thirteen. She wanted them each to have a special birthday celebration, but was on a tight budget and couldn't afford three major parties. She came up with the following solutions.

Her youngest was happy to just have family over to cut a homemade cake and sing Happy Birthday. Everyone wore party hats. Her eldest wanted a few friends to sleep over. They hired some videos, ordered pizza and gossiped half the night.

The seven-year-old was the one who wanted a traditional party the most. Margaret limited the number of invited friends to ten. She held the party in their backyard. With the help of her children, Margaret made a piñata, the cake and most of the snacks. They also made their own decorations and hats, an activity the two younger children delighted in. She limited the party to two hours' duration, providing a good balance between party games and simple playing time.

Everyone was happy and it didn't cost the earth.

FURTHER HELP

- Visit the website of the Child Accident Prevention Foundation of Australia (Kidsafe) at http://www.kidsafe.com.au for a fact sheet on selecting safe toys. Also try the Australian Toy Association site at http://www.austoy.com.au as well as some of the websites for various states' consumer affairs departments.

Useful books

Australian Consumer's Association 2003, *The Choice Guide to Baby Products*, 8th edn, Choice Books, Sydney.

Clegg, M. 2003, *Your Baby on a Budget*, New Holland Publishers, Sydney.

7

Back to work

The choice to return to paid work is not always easy. Many women feel torn emotionally between wanting to be full-time mothers and the need to earn an income. Others feel equally torn but for a different reason. While enjoying parenthood they crave the stimulation that work and career can bring, and feel guilty about wanting to go back.

Deciding whether and when to return to work is very personal. It will depend on social and lifestyle issues, your attitude to raising a family, your career aspirations and, of course, your financial position.

Some people claim that the cost of childcare is such that it's not worth going back to work: see Chapter 9, 'Childcare, nannies and babysitters' for an idea of the costs involved. Others argue that the harm to their long-term career, including missed promotion opportunities, makes it far more costly not to return. So who is right? Well, both, if that is their reasoned assessment of their personal circumstances. It's not possible to make a blanket statement that applies to everyone because each person's situation is unique.

There may be some ways to compromise and make your family–work balancing act slightly easier. Going back part-time or job sharing might be an option, as may telecommuting. You might be able to negotiate flexible working hours. Or you may even decide to take the plunge and start your own business, which is covered in the next chapter.

This chapter outlines your rights and options if and when you decide it's time to go back to paid work.

Some statistics

Does taking time off work to raise a family actually affect your career? In a study undertaken by the Human Rights and Equal Opportunities Commission, 54 per cent of women surveyed believe it does. A further 30.4 per cent said their careers took a backward step and 29.9 per cent of respondents went so far as to say they believed they sacrificed their careers when they had children.

Source: Human Rights and Equal Opportunity Commission, Pregnancy fact sheet, March 2001.

PARENTAL LEAVE

The term parental leave is a broad expression, encompassing maternity and paternity leave as well as adoption leave.

'Special' maternity leave is another type of leave, which may be available to help women who are recovering from a miscarriage, stillbirth, or pregnancy related illness. Paid sick leave might be available instead of unpaid special maternity leave in these circumstances.

Your rights

Rights to parental leave vary throughout Australia. Your entitlement might be established by federal or state legislation, or an award or agreement with your employer.

If you are unsure about your situation, check with your employer. Human resources departments in large businesses often have their policy in writing and you can ask for a copy. If you belong to a union you can raise the issue with your union representative or you can ask your state's industrial relations department.

Despite the variations, there are minimum entitlements that apply throughout Australia. Established by the federal *Workplace Relations Act 1996*, these minimum rights cannot be overridden or bargained away by any type of agreement. Your particular entitlements may be better, but they can't be lesser.

So what are these minimum rights?

Most employees are entitled to up to 52 weeks' unpaid parental leave. This is available to both mothers and fathers. If you both want to take some leave you're not entitled to 52 weeks each; that's the amount in total. Neither can you both take parental leave at the same time, except for one week around the birth or three weeks when a child is placed with you for adoption.

If you want to keep some money coming in while you're off work you can try combining annual or long service leave with your parental leave. However, your total period away from work can't be more than 52 weeks unless your employer agrees.

Your employer can hire someone else to do your job on a temporary basis in the meantime. When you return to work you're entitled to the same position you held before going on parental leave. If your old job no longer exists, you may be entitled to another job that is similar in pay and status.

Are you eligible?

To be eligible for the above minimum rights you generally need to have worked a continuous twelve months with your employer, either full-time or part-time. If you work on a seasonal or casual basis your position is less certain and needs to be checked, but you may still be eligible, particularly if you worked on a regular and systematic basis. If you have already taken parental leave, there's no need for you to work for another twelve months for that employer before being able to take parental leave again.

You don't need to be married or even living in a de facto relationship to be entitled to parental leave. There are no age restrictions.

Be sure to give your employer adequate notice of your intention to take leave. Do this in writing. Requirements and procedures vary under different laws, awards and agreements, and should be checked. Most likely you'll need to provide a medical certificate to confirm your pregnancy and due date. You may also need to provide a statutory declaration confirming your partner's intention to take paternity leave for more than one week, if relevant.

Note, there is nothing forcing you to take parental leave. You can apply to take any other type of leave you are entitled to instead, such as annual or long service leave. Indeed you aren't legally obliged to take any leave at all. If you are medically able and so inclined you may be able to return to work within a few days of the birth.

Paid maternity leave

While unpaid maternity leave is a widespread right, paid maternity leave is not. Some women are entitled to it under various agreements or individual contracts, but they are in the minority. Public servants generally have some entitlement, but the number of weeks of paid leave varies between states: generally ranging from two to twelve weeks.

If you take paid leave and then decide not to go back to work, you might find yourself having to pay the money back. It depends on the terms and conditions, so be sure to check.

Currently there's a significant push to introduce paid maternity leave for all Australian women. Various bodies including women's groups, some political parties, and the Australian Council of Trade Unions are trying to introduce laws. The Human Rights and Equal Opportunities Commission made an inquiry into paid maternity leave and came up with a proposal. Models reflect basic factors contained in an International Labour Organisation resolution—where eligible women would be entitled to up to fourteen weeks' paid leave. This would be at a rate of up to the federal minimum wage. The leave would be funded by the government, with employers being encouraged to top-up the benefits.

It is still early days for paid maternity leave, but the issue is certainly worth keeping an eye on.

BACK TO WORK OPTIONS

How do people manage to go back to work after parental leave and still spend time with their family?

In a recent report the Australian Bureau of Statistics investigated the type of work arrangements being used by parents in an attempt to balance work and family responsibilities. The following graph illustrates one of their findings. It is reproduced with the kind permission of the Australian Bureau of Statistics.

Figure 7.1: The type of work arrangement used to care for children

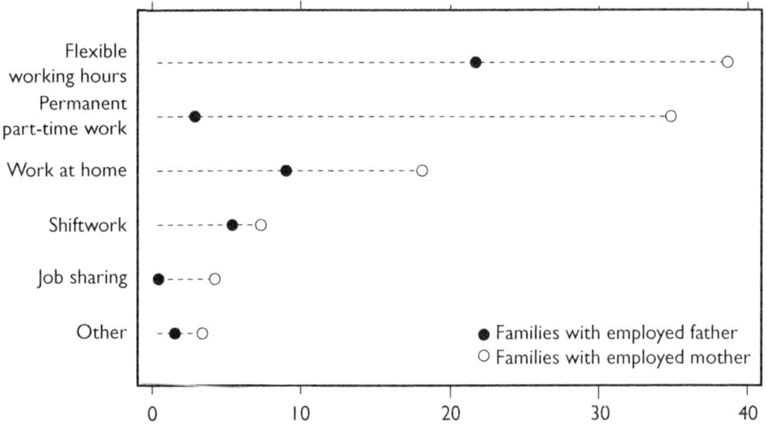

Source: Australian Bureau of Statistics 2002, Child Care Australia, Catalogue Number 4402.0, Canberra

The graph shows that it's mostly women who perform the juggling act with work and childcare. Seventy per cent of employed mothers make use of work arrangements to help with child rearing duties, compared to 30 per cent of employed fathers. The most popular method for women is flexible working hours (39 per cent), closely followed by permanent part-time work (35 per cent). Of course there's some overlap here, as many women have part-time/flexible hour jobs.

Where employed men do take on a childcare role, the vast majority (22 per cent) do this by the use of flexible working hours. Very few work part-time, and only a tiny proportion job share. Shiftwork is relatively popular with both sexes, and many couples coordinate their shifts to share family responsibilities.

Part-time work

Going back part-time suits many women, particularly in the early years while their children are still very young. It keeps some income coming in and helps maintain skills and contacts, while still allowing time with the child. It's not necessarily an easy option, but it does help maintain some balance.

How could it work for you? It depends on your personal needs and the business needs of your employer. Do you want to work a few full days a week and then have the other days off? Shortened days every day? Or shortened days a few days a week, with the rest off? Do you want permanent part-time, or do you intend to return full-time at a later date?

Discuss your options with your employer. If there is no provision for part-time work in your award or agreement you might nevertheless be able to negotiate a suitable arrangement.

Discrimination in the workplace

Anti-discrimination laws exist to protect working women. Details vary between states, but generally you cannot be discriminated against because of your parental status or family responsibilities.

You can't be dismissed purely because of your role as a parent. Depending on state laws, it may also be unlawful for you to be demoted, forced to work part-time against your will, denied promotion opportunities or disadvantaged in any way on the sole basis of your family status. Poor performance might lead to negative outcomes, but it must be the real reason and not a pretext.

Some case law suggests that employers who refuse to let women work part-time after maternity leave might be unlawfully discriminating. It all depends on the surrounding circumstances. Does part-time work fit within the reasonable needs of the business and is your employer prepared to give it a fair go? If you think you're the victim of discrimination, contact your union or an anti-discrimination body. Working women's centres and community legal centres can also advise you of your rights.

Job sharing

Another option, similar to part-time, but when it comes to job sharing, you are doing just that. You and another person are splitting a full-time position between you. The pay is divided based on the number of hours/days worked.

Different systems exist. You might have shared responsibility for the same duties, meaning one picks up where the other left off. This can be good for ongoing tasks that need someone there each day, but can cause potential difficulties. If the person you're job sharing with doesn't pull their weight, you might end up doing virtually a full-time job compressed into a few days.

Another method is to have divided responsibility. Here workers have their own projects and/or clients. They might provide backup support for each other when necessary, but other than that there is little overlap between their tasks.

It all comes down to what suits the business needs of the employer, as well as the needs of the staff.

Making it work

Natalia is a public service lawyer who job shares. She works a three-day week while her co-sharer Carol works two days. They share responsibility for the same clients. Natalia discovered both positive and negatives in the job sharing arrangement. She appreciates Carol's expertise and values the extra check on her decisions. There was the odd harrowing occasion, however, where Carol failed to communicate developments, causing Natalia considerable embarrassment in front of their clients. Putting up with personality quirks is another difficulty she encountered, particularly when it comes to tidiness and work methodology.

Natalia found that to make job sharing work, it's important to:

- not attempt to carry the whole job;
- prioritise work tasks;
- keep your own space—separate cupboard space and separate drawers; and
- keep each other up-to-date on developments.

Telecommuting

It may be possible to work from home while still being an employee. Telecommuting involves working in your own home-based office and keeping in touch with your employer using telecommunications technology. This can include a telephone, fax, and a modem link on a computer. You might need to provide your own equipment or your employer might provide it for you.

You might be required to go into your employer's office on a regular basis, and you might need to attend meetings. You might have set working hours, or you might simply be obliged to work until each given task or project is completed.

However, not all jobs are suited to telecommuting. Telecommuting is more likely to work for tasks that have a high degree of independence. Project work, research, analysis, writing, editing and some types of product development and creation may be suitable. But if your job depends on direct interaction with others or significant levels of supervision, it may not work. Similarly, if you need to go to the employer's premises often— for instance to look up files that can't be taken home—telecommuting might not be a viable option.

Employees, also, must be suited. Are you an independent worker? Can you meet deadlines and are you self-disciplined? The more self-motivating you are, the more likely it is that telecommuting will succeed.

Depending on the circumstances, your employer may not want you to use telecommuting as a substitute for childcare. And you yourself might find it hard to work when your child has passed the napping stage. The older they get, the less they sleep, and it is virtually impossible to work when your wide-awake child is demanding your attention. But even if you do need to make additional arrangements for children who are too young for school, at least you have the advantages of cutting commuting times and being close at hand. And by keeping a foot in the door, it can make it easier to go back to traditional work structures at a later date.

Sorting out the conditions

While telecommuting, you should be entitled to the same wages and conditions as others performing the same tasks in the employer's office. Similarly, you should have the same opportunities regarding training and promotion. It is easy to be overlooked, however. Out of sight, out of mind. Try to maintain your profile by visiting the employer's office on a regular basis and keeping in contact by phone and email.

There are also legal requirements to be considered. Occupational health and safety standards may need to be satisfied regarding matters such as a suitable desk, chair, computer set-up and so forth. Sufficient lighting, power points and clear exits are also important considerations.

Then there is the question of personal liability. What would happen if you hurt yourself in your home office while working? Or if clients or colleagues who attend your home office become injured? Who would be liable, your employer or you? Ensure you know your position if things go wrong, and find out whether you need to take out your own insurance.

After a long break

Re-entering the workforce after a long break to raise a family can be harrowing. Women who have been out of touch with an employer for many years often worry that their skills have become outdated. The thought of competing with younger colleagues only adds to the stress.

Labour market programs have been introduced by the federal government, helping to make the transition easier. Various programs exist and there may be one to suit you.

The 'Return to Work' program provides advice and training assistance for people who have been out of the workforce for at least two years as carers. The program can help with skills assessment, career and training plans. It can also help familiarise you with the latest advances in information technology—often the area that intimidates people the most. To find out if you are eligible call Centrelink Employment Services. If you are eligible, they may refer you to a Return to Work Managing Agent.

The JET (Jobs, Education and Training) program helps recipients of the Parenting Payment and certain other government benefits. The emphasis is on improving your long-term position through education and training. It can provide information, advice and make referrals to educational institutions, childcare services and state or local services. Help is offered with the development of a return to work plan. If you think you might be eligible, contact the Centrelink JET adviser.

A more recent initiative is the Transition to Work program. It helps parents, carers and people over 50 who are starting work for the first time or returning after an absence of at least two years. You do not have to be receiving income support to be eligible, but you do need to be looking for paid work. The package can include help with writing resumés and job applications, career counselling, and skills upgrade courses. It is delivered by a network of specialist service providers, which can be accessed via the Internet at http://www.workplace.gov.au or by calling the Transition to Work Enquiry Line.

FAMILY FRIENDLY EMPLOYERS

Balancing a family and a job can be very difficult, but there are ways employers can help make life run more smoothly. Lately there's an increasing recognition that employers should be taking active steps to become more family friendly, given the high number of working mothers.

If the following options are not already available in your workplace, consider raising the issue yourself.

Flexible working hours

Flexibility in the times employees start and finish work goes a long way. You can coordinate dropping off your child at school or with their carer with your starting and/or finishing time. And you have the opportunity to leave work early if your child needs medical attention or you want to attend a school function. Time can be made up on other occasions.

Personal/family leave

The ability to take paid leave to deal with personal or family issues—such as caring for sick children—is becoming more common. It means parents aren't obliged to use up their annual leave entitlement for such occurrences.

Occasional work from home

Even if you don't have a formal, long-term telecommuting arrangement, you might still be able to arrange the odd day where you work from home. This can be a godsend if your child is home ill or if your normal childcare arrangements fall through. It's best to discuss this possibility long before the need arises, rather than finding yourself uncertain in a crisis.

Access to telephone

A simple yet effective way to enable parents to keep in touch with those caring for their children.

Office crèches

Childcare facilities on employers' premises are very rare in Australia. They can be costly to establish and run, and compliance with regulations may not be easy. Even so, it's worth getting together with a few other parents and working out how to make a crèche viable. They may well be the way of the future.

Maintaining breastfeeding while working

This is perhaps the ultimate test of balancing work and family. Approach your boss, union, human resources department or equal opportunity officer for information on your workplace's breastfeeding policies. Not all employers leap with joy at the request, but it's up to you to be persistent and show them it can work. It's best to raise the issue well in advance, preferably before you go on maternity leave.

So how can it be done?

For a start, you will need a private room with a comfortable chair. This does not mean the toilets. Rather it is somewhere you can express milk safely with the help of a manual or electric breast pump—the latter being the faster option. You will need a fridge to store the expressed milk. Express during your breaks. If you need more time you may be able to arrange to make up the work time, perhaps at the end of the day.

If you employ a nanny, or a family member is looking after your child, it might even be possible for them to physically bring the child to you at work. The private room can then be used for direct feeding rather than expressing.

Another option is to have your childcare service close to your office, rather than your home. An office crèche would also help. You might be able to feed your baby personally during your breaks. In any case, you will cut travelling times and can give them a feed immediately before and after work.

FURTHER HELP

- Contact your state's industrial relations department for information on your rights as an employee. Also visit the website of the Human Rights and Equal Opportunities Commission at http://www.hreoc.gov.au.
- For information on labour market programs contact Centrelink on 136 150, Centrelink Employment Services on 132 850, or the Transition to Work Enquiry Line on 136 268. See also http://www.centrelink.gov.au and the Australian Employment Services website at http://www.workplace.gov.au.
- For tips on breastfeeding at work, see the website of the Australian Breastfeeding Association at http://www.breast feeding.asn.au.

Useful publications

Australian Breastfeeding Association 1999, *Breastfeeding, Women and Work*, revised edn, Australian Breastfeeding Association, Melbourne.

Benveniste, J. 1998, *Woman Work Child*, Simon & Schuster, Sydney.

O'Hanlon, M. and Morella, A. 2003, *Job Sharing: Two Heads are Better than One*, Allen & Unwin, Sydney.

Pocock, B. 2003, *The Work/Life Collision*, The Federation Press, Sydney.

8

Working from home

Ever been tempted to set off on your own? Keep your own hours, set your own pace, and keep your own profit?

In the previous chapter we looked at telecommuting as a back-to-work option. Telecommuting refers to working in a home-based office while still being someone else's employee. Here we're looking at establishing your *own* business that you run from home.

Many women start their own business not too long after having their children. Not only does it give them the flexibility to earn an income with a baby in tow, it often allows them to fulfil a long-held dream. Some see it as the ideal way to combine work and family; others simply have no choice. It's either that or face unemployment after being out of the work-force for a while. Whatever the impetus, you're most likely to succeed if you do your research and plan thoroughly.

As parents, we require the sort of arrangement that fits around our children's needs. The beauty of running your own business is that you can have your child at home with you as you work—and no-one can tell you not to. It may take a bit of juggling but the rewards are worth the effort.

EXAMINE YOUR MOTIVES

It's easy to be swept away by a dream, but you also need to be realistic. The purpose of a business, ultimately, is to make money. If you don't make the necessary profit it won't last long.

Running a business—even a home-based one—requires many hours of hard work. And as your baby grows out of the compliantly sleepy stage you'll find you have less time to work and will face more pressure. It's very hard to get work done when you're with an attention-demanding toddler. Sure, they'll go to childcare or school some time, but in the meantime expect to work late into the night or to get up in the wee hours. Even once your children do go on to childcare or school, your work days will be short and you'll have to contend with holidays.

You're probably saying 'but that's the whole point'. To be able to do both. Yes, it is, but keep in mind it won't necessarily be easy. And as to the question of profit, you may or may not earn as much money as you would as an employee. It's probable that in the early years at least, you will earn less than you would working for someone else. You need to ask yourself if you are prepared to make the trade-off.

Checklist—have you got what it takes?

Not everybody is suited to the challenges involved in running their own home-based business. The first requirement is an entrepreneurial personality with the ability to juggle family and work. Do you fit the bill?

- Do you thrive under stress or does it make you physically ill?
- If you suffer setbacks, do you pick yourself back up again— and again and again?
- Can you make plans yet be flexible enough to change direction quickly if unforeseen opportunities arise?
- Do you have the confidence to sell yourself and your product?
- Do you know your own worth and are you prepared to charge accordingly?
- Can you tailor your product or service to meet the needs of your market?
- Do you have childcare or babysitters lined up for when you need to attend meetings?
- Is there a time when you can make telephone calls without children vying for your attention?

- Can you follow-up on unpaid debts?
- Can you handle disputes with clients/customers effectively and without jeopardising your future relationship?

WHAT TYPE OF BUSINESS?

It can be anything from running a bed and breakfast, family daycare, selling cosmetics, hairdressing, fixing computers, interior decorating, to editing manuscripts. In fact, anything that can be done at home may be an option for your own business when you are raising young children.

Will you be starting a new business from scratch? It might be possible to buy an existing business that you can operate from your own home. If you buy an existing business you have the advantage of an established customer base, but you do need to pay for the goodwill. Or you might decide to sell the products of one of those operations that work by having people sell via parties and social connections. Find out whether you are obliged to buy a large selection of the products yourself first. It's possible you will not recoup the outlay.

Starting a new business from scratch is riskier but can be far cheaper. If you manage to hit on an original idea you may be in the enviable position of creating a new niche for yourself.

It will help if you've already worked in the area you are interested in. You already know how to create your product or service and most likely have ideas for improvement. You have contacts that might be useful in the future. Just be careful that you are not breaching any clauses in contracts with former employers that restrict you from setting up in competition. One relatively easy way to get started is to pick up some freelance work from a former employer. You know them; they know you. Once you get started you can branch out further.

Maybe you have a hobby that can be adapted—writing, illustrating, cooking, pottery and so forth. By the judicious use of marketing (working out who uses the product and why) and advertising, it's possible to turn a hobby into a viable business proposition.

If you don't have experience in your chosen field, don't let it deter you. Determination and drive are more important.

Doing what you enjoy, however, is essential. Before planning your own business, you need to identify your passion: something you feel strongly about and to which you are willing to devote time and energy. Working in an area you love will keep you going through the rough patches. A mere 'get rich quick' scheme will not.

GETTING STARTED

Do as much research as possible. Get to know your market, product or service, and know your competition. Attend workshops, courses and seminars—not just in your area of operation, but also in the nuts and bolts of how to run a small business.

Prepare a business plan. This detailed document describes your business proposal. It examines your business objectives, product profile, marketing plan, financial plan, and the repayment of any loans. A well structured business plan makes it easier to raise money from a financier if needed, and it's wise to employ the services of a professional accountant. If you don't need to borrow money, it's not a bad idea to create your own simple business plan anyway. It will help get you focused.

If you do need a loan or overdraft, consider your position carefully. Is this money you can afford to lose? Do you need to put your home up for collateral? Make sure you know precisely what you are risking.

Government assistance

If you receive specific types of Centrelink payments that include a living allowance component and you are registered with Centrelink as searching for full-time work, you might be eligible to apply for help via the New Enterprise Incentive Scheme (NEIS). This package of assistance includes an allowance for up to 52 weeks, training in small business management skills and business plan development, and business advice and mentorship during that all-important first year. Successful applicants are gauged on the merits of their business idea. The business must be assessed as commercially viable.

Self Employment Development (SED) is another option. To be eligible, you must be a job seeker who has been unemployed and receiving Newstart or Youth Allowance continuously for at least six months. SED allows you to concentrate on developing a business idea as an alternative to seeking a job.

State and territory government departments also offer services that promote and assist small businesses. Business Enterprise Centres and Small Business Services throughout Australia can provide you with information about workshops, courses, and grants.

Setting up shop

Working from home costs relatively little. You don't need to lease separate premises, and have no commuting costs. I'm assuming you won't need to hire staff, at least in the early days.

You might be lucky enough to have a spare room that you can convert into an office or workshop. If not you will need to be more creative. A kitchen table can double as a desk. Just be sure you have somewhere to lock valuable equipment away when not in use. A questing toddler's fingers can do much damage in no time at all. Obviously you need to keep any dangerous items safely locked up and out of reach.

The costs of setting up vary depending on the type of business. As a minimum most home offices require a computer, printer, fax, phone, photocopier, desk, chair and filing cabinet. This will put you back somewhere in the vicinity of $3000 to $5000. You may already have many of these items, so your initial outlay may be very low. Or you may decide to rent the equipment, especially if you have no other use for them—other than for the business.

In addition, you might need to purchase specialist craft equipment. Only buy what is essential at first; once you are more established you can think about upgrading.

Insurance

All businesses are subject to some degree of risk. You may need to take out various forms of business insurance—to cover the premises, equipment, stock, visitors to the premises and, of course, yourself. It's worth consulting an insurance broker.

MAKING IT LEGAL

Various formalities need to be considered. Give them serious thought before you start out, as your choices can have far reaching consequences.

Business structure

There are four basic types of small business structures:

Sole traders

If you run a business on your own, you will be classified as a sole trader. This is the case even if you hire employees. Sole traders carry unlimited liability for their business. This means that if your business incurs debts, you carry the full responsibility for meeting them, even to the extent that your personal assets can be seized. Sole traders pay tax on business earnings at their marginal tax rate and use their individual tax file number for income tax returns.

Partnerships

If you go into business with someone else you are entering a partnership, where profits and losses are shared. It's important to choose a business partner judiciously. The fact that you get along as friends or as a couple does not guarantee that a business relationship will work. Keep in mind that as a partner, you may be taking on unlimited liability not just for your own actions but also for those of your partner. A partnership needs its own unique tax file number.

Trusts

A small business can also be owned by a trust. A trust is a duty imposed on a person (the trustee) to hold income or property on behalf of others (the beneficiaries). Trusts have their own tax file numbers. Properly structured, they can offer capital gains tax savings and create income splitting opportunities. This is why they are popular with tax payers and unpopular with the tax office. Trusts are very complex so seek legal advice if you are considering using one as a small business structure.

Companies

A company is a separate legal entity, meaning it exists independently from its owners and will continue even if its owners die. It consists of shareholders (people who put money into the company) and directors (people who are in control of the overall direction the company takes). This is a complex structure and it can be time consuming and expensive to comply with regulations. The main advantage is that shareholders' liability is limited to the amount they invested in the business. As a director, however, you might have to provide a personal guarantee when borrowing money—which virtually puts you back into square one. If you are considering this type of business structure be sure to seek financial and legal advice.

Business names

You may need to register a business name in the state or territory in which you operate. If you are a sole trader or partnership and simply use your own name/s as your business name, registration is not necessary. If you use something different or a variation on your name—such as Sonia's Sewing Services—registration is compulsory. The purpose of registration is to identify the legal owners of the business. Registration must be completed before you start trading.

You need to check that the name you have selected is not already in use. You can do this for free at any Australian Securities and Investment Commission (ASIC) business centre or on their website at http://www.asic.gov.au. It's best to have a few alternative names in mind in case your first choice is not available.

Licences and approvals

You may also need to comply with various state and local government licensing and approvals regulations. Some revolve around the impact your business could have on your surrounding area. For instance, issues such as parking, energy use, pollution and noise can be relevant. To find out more, contact your local council and your state's business licence information service.

Your trade or profession may also impose its own requirements; for instance lawyers must have appropriate tertiary legal qualifications and the right type of practising certificate from the Law Society.

Registering under the tax system

Since 1 July 2000, Australia has had a new tax system that has drastically altered the way we do business.

But are you actually running a business or merely engaged in a hobby? The answer is not always obvious for new home-based operations, and can involve issues including size, scale and permanency, repetition and regularity. If you are uncertain seek advice from the ATO or a government small business advisory service.

The following matters apply to businesses, not hobbyists.

You should apply for an Australian Business Number (ABN). This is an identifying number that businesses use when dealing with one another and with government bodies. You must put your ABN on your tax invoices. If you don't have an ABN, any payments made to your enterprise may have withholding tax of 48.5 per cent deducted. Similarly, if your business buys goods or services from a supplier who does not quote an ABN, you will need to withhold some of the payment.

Also consider registering for the Goods and Services Tax (GST). You must have an ABN in order to register.

The GST is a broad based tax of 10 per cent on the sale or supply of most goods and services sold within Australia. It is charged at every step of the supply chain, meaning that registered businesses must include GST in their prices. Registration is compulsory if your business's annual turnover is over $50 000. If less, registration is optional. If you are GST registered, you're generally able to claim a credit for the GST component of business expenses.

The Pay As You Go (PAYG) system is the method used for reporting and paying tax on business income and withholding amounts. GST registered businesses do this by using Business Activity Statements; others use Instalment Activity Statements. PAYG instalments are generally made quarterly, but can be made annually if you meet the relevant criteria. The ATO will notify you if you are eligible to pay annually.

It's a good idea to attend a free BizStart seminar run by the ATO. The seminars provide you with a basic understanding of the tax issues and obligations that apply to small businesses. They are held in all major cities and in some large regional areas. For details call a BizStart co-ordinator on 1300 661 104.

BALANCING BUSINESS AND FAMILY

Running a business from home can be isolating. Spending hours (if not days) on end in the same house seeing no-one except for the members of your own immediate family can get to you. Introducing some balance is important. It keeps you happy, your family happy and allows you to be a productive business operator.

When do you work? When do you make phone calls, meet with clients or customers, and chase up new business opportunities? When are you Mum or Dad? And when are you just plain old you, with time to indulge in some relaxation or hobbies?

Time management

This is what it really comes down to. Being organised. It is best to make yourself a timetable and stick to it.

The timetable can be as detailed as you like. Include the hours you intend to work, taking into consideration your family duties such as dropping your kids off to childcare or school. Include time to spend with your family doing things that you all enjoy. And try to incorporate some 'you' time: time for an exercise class or a walk; time to meet up with friends; or time simply to relax with your partner. Ideally, you need some time to yourself each day, but this can be very difficult with a young family. Many parents sacrifice some sleep to get it.

You also need some sort of longer-term planner: a schedule to allow you to keep track of appointments, deadlines and due payments. Failure to keep to these schedules can soon spell the end of a home business.

Be organised, but be flexible. Build in enough slack to allow for the unexpected. You could fall ill or your child might succumb to one of the many childhood illnesses, putting you out of action for several days. If you haven't built enough flexibility into your schedule, you could miss future opportunities, look unprofessional or—in many cases—both.

Around the clock

Connie is a writer. Her three-year-old son Leon attends daycare from Monday to Wednesday. Connie cannot fit all of her work into those three days, but she doesn't like the idea of having her son in daycare every day. Leon dropped his day sleep several months ago, and is so demanding it's impossible for her to get any work done when they are together. She quickly learnt that she shouldn't even try. Her work output was poor and her son became very distressed.

On her son's home days, Connie gets up at 4 am and puts in two to three hours before her son awakes. Outside of those hours, she restricts herself to emails if she needs to contact someone, rather than take the chance that a very unprofessional wailing will cut through her phone calls. If she receives a call she makes her excuses, settles Leon with a favourite activity, and only then returns the call. Meetings and library research trips are scheduled for daycare days.

Any unfinished work gets tackled on the weekend, when her husband is available to take Leon off her hands. But what about time for herself and her partner? Leon goes to bed at 7.30 pm, allowing Connie a little time to unwind, recharge her batteries, and spend time with her husband.

Connie makes sure she only commits herself to deadlines that she is certain she can achieve. She always schedules herself to complete a project before the deadline, in case something ends up delaying her unexpectedly.

FURTHER HELP

- The Business Entry Point website provides access to the whole range of federal, state and local government information, services and transactions for small business operators. Visit it for links to websites regarding government assistance, business names, licences and approvals and more. See http://www.business.gov.au.
- For information on employment programs and services (including self-employment) for Centrelink customers, call Centrelink on 136 150. Also visit the Australian Employment Services website at http://www.workplace.gov.au.
- For information on the tax treatment of your business and for information on registering under the new tax system see the Australian Taxation Office website—http://www.ato.gov.au. You can also call the business Tax Reform Infoline on 132 478.

Useful publications

English, J. 2003, *How to Organise and Operate a Small Business in Australia*, 9th edn, Allen & Unwin, Sydney.

Heilbuth, D. 2001, *Earning Money from Home*, Choice Books, Sydney.

Ryan, A. 2002, *GST and BAS for Dummies*, Wiley Publishing, Brisbane.

Williams, A. 2001, *So . . . You Want to Start Your Own Business?* McGraw Hill, Sydney.

9

Childcare, nannies and babysitters

Figures recently released by the Australian Bureau of Statistics show that nearly half of all Australian children aged under twelve attend some form of childcare, whether formal or informal.

Most parents said the main reason they used childcare was work-related. The next most common reason was that it was beneficial for the child. People using informal care (such as grandparents) emphasised personal motives.

The numbers using informal care are declining. This may be because some grandparents are too old to take on such a mammoth task, a consequence of our trend of delaying parenthood. And many grandparents have greater expectations of their retirement years than previous generations and want to maintain some of their freedom.

Chances are that at some stage you will need to consider formal childcare in some shape or form, either as a substitute for or in addition to informal care. There are many options but because this is such as crucial area, the choices are never easy. Be sure to examine all your avenues and do your research thoroughly. Your child's wellbeing depends on it.

Once again, the question of money comes into play. Finding the right option at the right price can be a challenge. This chapter looks at the financial aspects of childcare, nannies and babysitters, asks whether it is worth the outlay, refers to sources of assistance, and offers some money-saving tips.

Keep in mind that variations between states—even within states and cities—make it very hard to generalise about the costs of care. I've included some guidelines as to price to try to give you a broad idea but please don't take them as a substitute for your own research.

LONG DAYCARE

Long daycare is a popular choice for parents of children aged from birth to five/six years. As the name suggests, these centres are open for extended hours—often 7.30 am to 6 pm — but hours vary between centres. They can be run by local councils, churches, community groups or private small businesses.

All centres need to be licensed and must meet certain standards regarding size, staff–child ratio, health and safety. Regulations vary throughout Australia. The staff–child ratio varies depending on the child's age and the state you live in. For instance in New South Wales the ratio is one carer per five children for newborns to two-year-olds, one carer per eight children for two- to three-year-olds, and one carer to ten children for three- to six-year-olds. (These figures are currently under review.) In South Australia, for the under-two's the ratio is one unqualified carer per five children and one qualified carer per twenty children. Things get more complicated for children over two, particularly for mixed age groups.

Long daycare centres must register and participate in the Quality Improvement and Accreditation System, which covers areas such as the centre's activities and staff matters. The National Childcare Accreditation Council administers the system.

Choosing between long daycare centres is not easy. Visit as many as you can, preferably dropping in without warning so you can see how they function when they are not expecting you. Examine the physical environment. Is it clean, attractive and in good order? How do the carers interact with the children? Are they warm and encouraging, or are they often irritable and cross? Ask them about their policies on discipline, accidents, cuddles and so forth. What does their daily routine involve? Word of mouth is also a good way to choose, but it's not a substitute for your own investigation.

Usually your choice comes down to instinct. Hard to say exactly why, but often you get a gut feeling as to whether something is right for your child or not. Trust those feelings.

Remember that waiting lists can be very long (several months or even a couple of years) and you should put your child's name down as soon as possible. If you want to place a baby in daycare, consider going on the list before the baby's even born!

Typical costs

And now the question of cost. Rates vary significantly, but you can expect to pay between $30 and $60 a day, even more in affluent areas. At an average of say $45 a day, you're looking at $225 for a five-day week. Many centres charge the full daily rate even if you take your child in late and pick him or her up early.

Rates often vary within centres according to the age of your child. Younger children need more attention and so costs are generally highest for those aged under two. Rates can drop for two- to three-year-olds, then drop again for the four- to five-year-olds.

If your child is sick you still need to pay for missed days. Some centres offer make-up days for public holidays, others don't.

Cutting costs

Shop around and compare the prices of a few local centres. Look at some near your home and some near your place of work—the difference might surprise you.

Some centres provide food. Naturally they cost more, and you need to decide whether the extra cost is worth the time you save preparing lunches in the morning. Some charge you for nappies, other allow you to provide your own. All these sorts of factors need to be weighed up.

Be sure to look into your eligibility for Child Care Benefit. It can significantly reduce the amount you pay for long daycare fees. If eligible, you can claim the benefit in different ways: as a reduction in the fees that you pay to the centre or as a lump sum payment from the Family Assistance Office after the end of the financial year. For details see Chapter 10, 'Government assistance'.

FAMILY DAYCARE

Unlike long daycare, family daycare takes place in the carer's own home. If you are keen on a home environment for your child, this might be the option for you.

Carers are organised in networks known as family daycare schemes. The schemes can be run by varying bodies: local councils, churches, non-profit community groups, or private businesses.

All carers must be licensed. Certain criteria have to be met on issues including insurance, safety standards, first aid training, and police checks on all residents of the house. Only small numbers of children can be taken on, usually up to a maximum of seven at any given time. Laws regulate the mix of ages.

Your first port of call is usually your local council, who can provide you with contact details for your local family daycare scheme. Or you can call the National Family Day Care Council on 1800 658 699. The scheme's coordination unit will discuss your needs and help you find a suitable carer. You are put in touch with those that have vacancies, then it's up to you to select the one you think is best for your child.

Family daycare is more flexible than long daycare and can suit shift workers. Overnight care might even be available. Before and after school care may also be an option, but the difficulties involved in transporting children about makes many carers reluctant to take on this task. Raise the issue if desired—especially if you have a younger child with the carer. Parents who are on call and find it hard to predict their working hours might also benefit from family daycare, and should discuss their requirements with the carer. Keep in mind that regulations limiting the numbers of children cared for at any given time might make it hard for you to have your child cared for in an emergency.

Typical costs

Rates vary between schemes. Charges are levied by the hour, but many schemes require you to pay for a minimum number of hours per day (often six). After hours rates are generally higher than business hour rates. Depending on where you live, you could be paying in the vicinity of $3 to $5 per hour. If you use eight hours of care a day, five days a week, you could be paying something like $120 to $200 a week. Food and nappies are generally not provided.

Cutting costs

Generally speaking, family daycare is a cheaper option than long daycare. You do need to shop around, of course, and consider your overall needs as well as the money issue. Contact the Family Assistance Office to discuss your eligibility for the Child Care Benefit, discussed in the following chapter.

PRESCHOOLS/KINDERGARTENS

Preschools (also known as kindergartens in some states) are for children turning four, but differences in cut-off dates cause variations in starting ages. Preschools tend to operate on the same calendar as government schools, in other words they close during school holidays, a good twelve weeks or so of the year. Their hours of operation are limited, usually 9 am to 3 pm but this can vary. Many only offer enrolments on a two- or three-day basis. Some pre-schools have longer operating hours and accept younger children, and are in effect a combined preschool/daycare. But, generally, they may not suit parents who work full-time, at least not as the sole source of childcare. Preschools can be the right option if you also have a child at school and you work on a part-time or casual basis to fit in with school hours.

Preschools can be run by churches, local councils and non-profit community groups. The department of education in your state may also run some preschools, and some private schools offer preschool or 'preparatory' services.

Typical costs

Prices vary yet again, to the point where guidelines are virtually pointless. In some states fees are charged, elsewhere voluntary contributions are made. Preschools attached to the public education system may be free, but are more common in some states (for instance Queensland) than others. Not surprisingly, preschools run by private schools cost the most.

In any case, preschools tend to be cheaper than long daycare, partly because their operating hours are shorter. And as they are closed during school holidays, you aren't required to pay fees for those weeks of the year.

Cutting costs

As always, the first rule is to shop around. Compare prices and all the other non-monetary factors that come into play when making your decision.

You might be able to get a refund on a proportion of the fees paid to the preschool under the Child Care Benefit scheme. This is not the same as having fees reduced up front, as may be possible for long daycare and family daycare users. See the following chapter for more details about the operation of Child Care Benefit.

Some preschools also offer fee relief to those families who have trouble meeting the costs. In New South Wales, for example, families earning under $40 794 (at the time of writing) can apply for fee relief. Contact the preschool directly for details.

OFFICE CRÈCHES

A very small number of employers provide childcare facilities for staff on their premises. The reasons for this rarity are the cost of establishing and running the crèche, lack of space, and the difficulty in complying with the necessary regulations. It's worth getting together with a few other parents, working out how to make a crèche viable, and lobbying your employer. Issues to research include the fringe benefit tax treatment of work-based childcare. You also need to consider whether you will need to pay for the service and if so, how? Would it be possible to deduct the costs from your pre-tax salary? And would it ultimately end up being cheaper to use the more traditional forms of care?

BEFORE AND AFTER SCHOOL CARE

The juggling act doesn't end when your children start school. Unless you work on a part-time or casual basis (or happen to be a teacher), you may need outside hours school care.

These services offer care before and/or after school hours for primary and early secondary school students, and many provide care on pupil-free days. If you're a full-time employee with the standard four weeks' annual leave, chances are you'll need some vacation care as well.

Most services are run on the school's premises. Both public and private schools may offer this service. Raise the issue with the school staff who can provide you with the service's contact details.

Some long daycare centres also offer outside school hours service. You drop off and pick up your child at the centre, and the centre transports the children to and from the schools. Usually school children are kept separate from the younger children attending the centre. This arrangement can be convenient if you have both a child in daycare and a child at school. Not many centres offer this service, however, and even with those that do your options may be limited as they only have arrangements with certain schools.

Typical costs

Depending on the service you could be paying around $7 to $15 for a morning session, $9 to $17 for afternoons. If you need both before and after school care, five days a week, a figure of $100 per week is not unreasonable. This is for one child. Vacation care also adds to the financial strain, and can cost about $30 to $50 per day, but again, prices fluctuate between services.

Cutting costs

Some outside hours school care services are more expensive than others. But as most are attached to the schools children attend, there is little or no scope to shop around. You could try centres situated away from the schools, but they are often more expensive.

Before hours care tends to be marginally cheaper than after hours care, so you might be able to shuffle your working hours to take advantage of this. The service might offer both permanent and casual bookings, the former being cheaper and offering one of the few true opportunities to save.

You can try lessening the amount of formal care you actually need—not by cutting back on your working hours, but by sharing pick-ups with other parents who attend your child's school. Not only does this save money, it can also ease the pressure on your child. Using both before and after school care can make for a very long day (potentially 7.30 am to 6 pm), which can be particularly hard on younger children.

Financial assistance via the Child Care Benefit may also be an option and is well worth investigating. More information can be found in the next chapter.

NANNIES

Previously the exclusive province of the rich, nannies are becoming a more common option. If you have a few children, the prices can actually be competitive.

Nannies provide one-on-one attention in your own home. Usually they take on sole responsibility for the kids while you are at work. Their duties can include bathing and dressing the children, keeping their bedrooms tidy, preparing their meals, taking them to school and back, and supervising homework and recreational activities.

Now the hard part. How do you find a good nanny? There are no licensing requirements as there are for daycare providers. Rather it's a matter of experience and personality. Check for first aid qualifications. If a candidate claims to have completed a relevant course, look into it further. Is it one of those expensive private six-week nanny courses or a proper childcare certificate offered by a recognised tertiary institution?

There are two ways to search for a nanny—find one yourself (for instance by word of mouth or by advertising) or use a recruitment agency. Some agencies charge a placement fee and then leave you to negotiate ongoing prices with the nanny. Others charge yearly service fees and set the rates that the nanny can charge.

Either way, it can still be a harrowing experience. The trust you place in a nanny is tremendous, and you absolutely have to be sure that she (people rarely choose men) is the right person. Ask about her views on child rearing in general, and her approach to discipline. Ask how she would handle a few specific emergency situations. Look into her employment history. Check her identity and follow-up on references. Do you have any other requirements? For instance, must she be a non-smoker? Must she be able to tolerate your pet Doberman and so forth? The nanny must also click with your children. Introduce them (preferably without saying 'this might be your nanny') and watch how they interact.

Keep in mind that hiring a nanny can generate responsibilities for you as an employer. You may need to take out domestic workers' compensation insurance (relatively inexpensive, usually under $50 per year) and you might need to pay super-annuation on the nanny's behalf (9 per cent of her income). Nannies are entitled to four weeks' annual leave and five days a year sick leave. Tax issues also arise, such as issuing tax sum-maries and paying the nanny's tax to the ATO. If you hire a nanny through an agency and the nanny is actually employed by the agency rather than by you, some of these issues may not arise. This option may well cost more, however, and you need to consider the trade off between cost and convenience.

Typical costs

So, what's a reasonable price? Going rates for full-time nannies are $16 to $18 per hour; for part-time nannies employed on a permanent basis, you could be paying $16 to $20 per hour. You could easily be looking at $350 to $800 a week for a qualified nanny. Very experienced nannies can charge even more. Live-in nannies tend to be a bit cheaper. Because they are saving money on rent and food, they can afford to charge less.

Say you work full-time and have three children: two in long daycare and one using before and after school care. You could still be paying around $400 to $700 a week in care fees, and not enjoying the convenience and extra services a nanny provides. Suddenly nannies don't sound too expensive, do they? Do your comparisons before you decide.

Cutting costs

Unlike the previous types of childcare, here there is significant scope for saving money. As mentioned, a live-in nanny tends to be a bit cheaper but you also need to have the room to house him/her properly. And of course you might not want someone there at all hours.

Consider using a nanny on a part-time or casual basis only. Discuss your requirements with the nanny or agency to see if this is feasible. Alternatively, you might decide to share a nanny with another family. Not only does this reduce costs, it provides playmates for your children. You will need to work out details such as whose home will be used and how you split the charges.

Nannies can become registered carers for the purposes of the Child Care Benefit (see the next chapter), meaning you might be able to claim a refund on a proportion of the fees paid to the nanny.

BABYSITTERS

Here we're looking at someone to mind the children for a few hours while you go out for a well-earned break. Or a medical appointment. Or a job interview. Whenever you need someone to mind the children and have no other form of care available.

Babysitters generally mind your children in your own home, and on night outings put them to bed. Again, they need to be someone you can trust implicitly. Other than that, anyone can be a babysitter. It can be the teenager from down the street. It can be a friend or relative. It can be an experienced nanny hired on an hourly basis, or someone hired through a babysitter's agency. Babysitter agencies can hire out a bit of a mix: experienced nannies, less experienced girls starting out in childcare and mums who are after a bit of additional income. Specify your needs when you call them. If your child attends formal childcare, consider asking the carers whether they also perform private babysitting duties and how much they charge.

Occasional childcare centres are an alternative to day time babysitters. Many are situated near shopping centres so you can have your child minded while you shop. They can be used for other purposes too, of course. You may be able to make bookings on a regular or casual basis, the former generally charged at a lower rate. Some long daycare centres also offer occasional care.

And you'll probably come across various facilities that have their own crèches, such as gymnasiums and swimming pool centres. Crèche operating hours are usually rather limited. Some facilities charge for crèche services, some don't.

Typical costs

An experienced nanny hired by the hour would cost the most. Depending on the agency you could be paying $20 or more per hour for casual rates, and there's likely to be a minimum number of hours charged: usually three or four. Less experienced babysitters hired through babysitting agencies might be a few dollars per hour cheaper. Agency prices tend to be higher during the day than at night, the logic being that the little darlings sleep at night so there's less work to be done. Agencies might charge loadings for particularly large families.

But what if you're happy to use a young relative, friend or neighbour? How much should you offer to pay them? This depends on your budget and your relationship. Discuss the matter with them and work out a figure that you are both satisfied with. Once you know what the professionals charge, you can adjust downwards accordingly.

Cutting costs

If you have access to a doting grandparent, you're likely to be able to have your children minded for free. But assume that's not an option. What other ways can you save money without jeopardising your children's safety and wellbeing?

Are there any babysitting groups in your local community? Sometimes bands of parents get together and work out an informal roster system where they agree to mind each other's children. Make enquiries at playgroups, church groups, mothers groups and other community groups.

If there aren't any around or at least none that you feel comfortable with, consider forming your own. It needn't be large. You might just come to an arrangement with a few close friends or relatives. It will cost you nothing; just be sure you are prepared to reciprocate.

IS CHILDCARE WORTH THE COST?

This is not a simple calculation. You can't just plug numbers into a formula and have the answer.

Say you want to take on a job where you earn $500 a week. You look into various childcare options and the one that suits you the most costs $200 a week, taking into account the Child Care Benefit. Now you effectively earn $300 a week, less really, once you take into account meals, transport and so forth.

Is that worth it?

What if you end up with $200 a week, $400 or $600 a week? Would any of these figures make childcare worthwhile?

You're probably saying it depends. It depends on how much your partner earns and how much you need the money. It depends on whether you want to work or whether you prefer to be an at-home parent. Will you be happy, will your child be happy? And how can you weigh such considerations against financial matters anyway? They are totally different quantities.

The fact is that people do make such judgements. They have to. For some people the answer is obvious; for others it involves a great deal of soul searching.

You are the only person who can make the decision. The checklist below provides some suggestions for the financial considerations only. How you weigh these up against your life choices and desires is up to you!

Checklist—financial considerations

- As a starting point, subtract childcare fees and other work related expenses from your anticipated earnings. How does the net figure look?
- If you go back to work, what will the impact be on any government assistance that you currently receive or expect to receive in the future? Factor that potential loss into your estimated net earnings.
- If you don't go back, can you live comfortably enough on just your partner's earnings?
- Do you have a buffer such as insurance in case your partner unexpectedly loses their ability to earn an income, either temporarily or permanently?
- Can you maintain effective savings and investment plans on one income?
- Are you on parental leave? If you resign now and take a few years off to raise your family, would it be easy for you to find another job in the future?
- If you received paid parental leave and then don't return to work, do you need to repay the money?
- Is part-time or casual work an option, if only so you can keep your foot in an employer's door?
- If you take a break from work, what would the effect be on your career in the long-term? Consider missed promotion opportunities and forgone salary increases.
- If you delay returning to work, how will forgone employer-contributed superannuation affect your retirement?

FURTHER HELP

- Your local council can provide you with a list of long daycare services, family daycare and preschools in your area.
- The Child Care Access Hotline can provide you with information about the availability of childcare services in your area. Call 1800 670 305. Or you can call the National Family Day Care Council on 1800 658 699 for the phone number of your local family daycare scheme.
- The National Childcare Accreditation Council administers quality assurance systems for long daycare centres, family daycare schemes and outside school hours care. Visit their website for general information and for help selecting a service. See http://www.ncac.gov.au.
- The Family Assistance Office can give you information about the Child Care Benefit—call 136 150.

10

Government assistance

The federal government offers financial assistance to many Australian families. There is a wide range of benefits available to suit different families' circumstances. Maybe you don't qualify, maybe you do. It's worth looking into.

The Family Assistance Office, a relatively new body, administers most payments that help with the costs of raising a family. Offices are located in Centrelink Service Centres, as well as some Medicare offices and Australian Taxation Office (ATO) sites. However there are some payments, for instance the Parenting Payment, that you can only get through Centrelink.

TYPES OF GOVERNMENT ASSISTANCE

The following is a general description of the types of government assistance available at the time of writing. Figures quoted are for the financial year 2003/04. Naturally these are subject to change, as indeed are the types of payments themselves. Visit the Centrelink or Family Assistance Office websites for updated details. For information on your personal situation, be sure to contact the relevant body directly to discuss your eligibility.

Family Tax Benefit (FTB) Part A

Paid by the Family Assistance Office, this provides help with the cost of raising children. To qualify you must have a dependent child under 21 or a dependent full-time student aged 21 to 24.

Your child must not be receiving Youth Allowance. As with

virtually all payments, you must satisfy residency requirements and an income test.

If your family income is less than $31 755 you receive the maximum rate of FTB Part A, which varies depending on the number of children you have and their ages. The cut-out point at which you're not entitled to any benefit at all also varies depending on the number of children you have and their ages. There's no point reproducing long lists of figures that date rapidly, so we'll just consider one example to give you a vague sort of idea. If you have two children under eighteen and none over, the cut-out is $92 637. This figure increases with number and age.

Family Tax Benefit (FTB) Part B

Also paid by the Family Assistance Office, this provides extra assistance to families where there's one main source of income. Sole parents receive the maximum rate regardless of income. In the case of two-parent families, the primary earner's income isn't taken into account. The secondary (or lesser) earner can receive some FTB Part B if he or she earns under:

- $11 559 where the youngest child is under 5; or
- $8614 where the youngest child is 5 to 18.

Family Tax Benefit payment options

For FTB Parts A and B you have a few payment options. You can elect to have:

- fortnightly payments from the Family Assistance Office;
- a lump sum payment after the end of the financial year;
- one part paid fortnightly and the other part after the end of the financial year; or
- a claim through the ATO on lodgement of your tax return.

The ramifications of your choice are explained under the heading 'Risk of overpayment', near the end of this chapter.

Note that FTB Parts A and B are payments for the children, not the parents. Sounds like playing with words, but in essence this means payments aren't taxable and don't need to be included on your tax return.

Child Care Benefit (CCB)

This helps pay for the costs of childcare. Children born on or after 1 January 1996 must be immunised or have an approved exemption in order for parents to claim.

The amount of CCB you receive depends on various factors. Your income, the type and number of hours of care you use, and whether you use childcare for work related purposes determine what you get.

There are two types of care:

- approved care—which includes long daycare, family daycare, most before and after school care, most vacation care, and some occasional care services; and
- registered care—which includes some private preschools and some outside school care services. It may also include nannies and even friends or relatives that you pay to look after your child. Carers need to be registered with the Family Assistance Office.

The CCB isn't paid for carers who are neither approved nor registered.

The benefit rate is highest for low income families (currently those on a family income under $31 755) then drops as income rises. Those above the top income threshold (currently $98 710 if you have two children in childcare) might still receive the minimum rate, which is up to $23.00 a week for each child in care.

If you are eligible for CCB and use *approved* care, you can get the minimum Child Care Benefit for up to 20 hours of care a week regardless of your situation. To claim up to 50 hours a week for *approved* care you and your partner if you have one must both satisfy the work test. In other words, you are both either:

- working (including the self-employed and those on parental leave);
- studying or training;

- actively looking for work;
- volunteering for fifteen or more hours per week; or
- a person with a disability or caring for someone with a disability.

If work commitments require you to have your child in care for more than 50 hours per week, call the Family Assistance Office for details on whether you can claim the excess hours. To receive more than the minimum benefit for approved care you need to estimate your income and satisfy an income test.

If you use *registered* care, you are entitled to the benefit only if you and your partner both satisfy the above work test. This applies regardless of the number of hours claimed. The amount of benefit you receive for registered care does not depend on your income, so you do not need to estimate your income.

So how do you claim?

If you use *approved* care, you can have the CCB paid directly to the childcare service, meaning you get to pay reduced fees. Alternatively, you can choose to pay full fees and claim the benefit from the Family Assistance Office as a lump sum payment after the end of the financial year.

For those using *registered* care there's just one option. Pay full fees, collect your receipts and send them to the Family Assistance Office with the appropriate form. You can do this once the period you are claiming for has passed. You have up until twelve months after the care was provided to make your claim.

You cannot claim CCB through the ATO.

Maternity Allowance

This is a one-off payment from the Family Assistance Office of $822.72. The aim is to help with the costs of a new baby. To qualify you must be eligible for FTB Part A and either have:

- a newborn or care of a newborn within thirteen weeks of the birth;
- a child entrusted to your care for adoption within 26 weeks of birth; or
- a stillborn baby or a baby that dies shortly after birth.

You must claim through the Family Assistance Office before your baby is 26 weeks old. You can't claim this payment through the ATO.

Maternity Immunisation Allowance

Another one-off—this time $208. This is for children aged 18 to 24 months who are fully immunised, on a recognised catch-up schedule, or who have an approved exemption. You must have received the Maternity Allowance and/or be eligible for FTB Part A at the time of lodging the claim. If you have gone back to work and your combined income is therefore over the threshold, you will not get the Immunisation Allowance. You must lodge your claim with the Family Assistance Office before your child turns two and, again, you can't claim through the ATO.

Parenting Payment

The Parenting Payment is paid by Centrelink. There are two types of Parenting Payment—single and partnered. It provides extra help for low income families with a dependent child under sixteen. Assets tests also apply. Note this differs to the FTB, where income tests apply but there are no assets tests.

Sole parents can receive up to $440.30 a fortnight, partnered parents generally up to $342.80 a fortnight.

Unlike FTB, the Parenting Payment is a payment to the parents, as opposed to the children. The upshot of this is that payments are taxable and need to be included on the parents' tax returns.

Baby Bonus

If you had a baby or gained legal responsibility for a child aged under five after 30 June 2001, you may be eligible to claim the Baby Bonus. This is done through the ATO, not the Family Assistance Office. You can get the bonus even if you don't have any income or pay tax. Lodge your claim with your tax return, or send it to the ATO on its own if you don't need to lodge a return. You can claim each year until the child turns five.

It doesn't matter if you already have other children or if you are receiving other family benefits. And there's no upper limit on taxable income.

The amount you are entitled to is not straightforward.

The Baby Bonus is calculated on the basis of the tax you previously paid. Your income in the year you are claiming for is compared to your income in the 'base year'. The base year will be the year *before* you had the baby, unless you choose the year you had him or her. If you choose the year you had the baby, you have to wait another year before you can claim. Once you choose a base year, you can't change it.

If your income in the claim year is less than that in the base year, you may get some Baby Bonus. If your income in the claim year is $25 000 or less, your minimum bonus for a full year will be $500. (However, your payment may be less in the first year, as the bonus is calculated from the date of birth or the date you gained legal responsibility.)

But what if you had no income in the base year? You may still be entitled to a minimum bonus payment of $500 per year.

Usually it is the mother who receives the bonus. However, you can transfer your eligibility for the Baby Bonus to your partner (married or de facto). This could be worthwhile if your partner could get a higher bonus than you could—for instance, if their taxable income is less than $25 000 and yours is above that figure. To estimate what you're entitled to, visit the ATO website and use their Baby Bonus calculator.

Choosing a base year

Meredith and Ken had a baby on 12 September 2003. Meredith wasn't sure which year to use as her base year for the Baby Bonus. In 2002, the year before she had the baby, her income was $49 000. In 2003, the year of the birth, her income dropped to $36 000. Meredith stopped work shortly before she had the baby and planned to be on unpaid maternity leave for one year. After that she intended to go back to work part-time until her child reached school age. She expected to earn over $25 000 on a part-time basis.

Meredith used the ATO's online calculator. She found that if she used 2002 as her base year, the maximum bonus she could claim would be higher than if she used the lower income figure in 2003.

The amount she'd receive would be the highest in the year she earned no income. If by some chance she ends up earning $49 000 (the base year level of income) or more in any year, she will receive no Baby Bonus for that year. Once her child turns five, Meredith will no longer be eligible.

The Baby Bonus and your super

If you wouldn't otherwise be able to make a superannuation contribution (say because you haven't worked in the last two years) changes to the law mean you now can if you receive the Baby Bonus.

It's possible to make a personal super contribution in the twelve months after you receive the Baby Bonus. Funds aren't obliged to accept such contributions, however, so check with your particular fund.

The amount you can contribute can be more or less than the Baby Bonus.

Other government benefits

Other benefits might apply:

- Large Family Supplement—for those getting FTB for four or more children, this supplement is paid for the fourth and subsequent children.
- Multiple Birth Allowance—for families receiving FTB who

have triplets, quads, quintuplets and so on! Payable until the children turn six.

- Rent assistance—extra help for those who pay rent to private landlords as opposed to public housing rent. You need to receive more than the base rate of FTB Part A.
- Assistance for Isolated Children—where the child cannot go to a government school because they live too far away.
- Carer Allowance (Child)—for a person looking after a child with a disability or severe medical condition. There are no income and assets tests.
- Double Orphan Pension—where both parents or adoptive parents are dead, or one is dead and the other cannot be found or is in an institution on a long-term basis.
- Health Care Card—if you receive the maximum FTB Part A fortnightly or the Parenting Payment (Partnered).
- Pensioner Concession Card—for those on the Parenting Payment (Single).

Through the maze

Alison and Wayne were both professionals on high incomes, each earning over $100 000 per annum. They had recently had a child and Alison had resigned from her job. She decided to work on a freelance basis for a few years, mainly to maintain her work contacts. Her income the first year was around $9000. They did not expect to receive any government assistance but their accountant advised them that Alison may be eligible for FTB Part B, where only her income was taken into account. Alison lodged a claim with her tax return and found she was entitled to a small lump sum. She decided against applying for the FTB as fortnightly payments as her income was liable to fluctuate too markedly. She was also entitled to the Baby Bonus.

In contrast, Shelley and Steven's combined income was $50 000 per year. Shelley took six months off work then returned on a part-time basis, placing her child in family daycare two days a week. Their new combined income was $32 000 per year. They were entitled to FTB Parts A and B (which they elected to take on a fortnightly basis), the CCB (taken as reduced fees), the Maternity Allowance and (eventually) the Maternity Immunisation Allowance. Their assets were too high to allow them to receive any Parenting Payment, but they were entitled to Rent Assistance. Shelley was also entitled to the Baby Bonus.

CLAIMING ASSISTANCE

Eligibility for government assistance

Tests differ depending on the type of payment sought, but some basic conditions must be met to establish eligibility. To check your eligibility, you should contact the Family Assistance Office or Centrelink directly to discuss your personal circumstances. Contact details are at the end of this chapter.

Australian residency

An Australian resident is someone whose normal place of residence is in Australia, and who is an Australian citizen or a permanent resident. Actual residency requirements vary between payments: it may suffice to be the holder of certain visas. In many cases you need to be present in Australia to receive payments.

Income and assets tests

To qualify for assistance you may need to satisfy an income test, which varies from payment to payment. Normally, maximum rates are paid to those whose income is below a certain amount. As income levels increase, entitlements are reduced. If you earn over a certain amount you may be ineligible to receive support, but keep in mind that thresholds often increase with the number of dependent children you have.

Some assets tests also apply for certain payments from Centrelink, but there is no assets test for any of the payments from the Family Assistance Office.

Couples

Your partner's financial situation may also be taken into consideration. In other words, often your combined family income is the key to your eligibility. This doesn't just apply to married couples, but also to those living in a de facto relationship.

Making a claim

To claim a benefit you need to fill in the relevant forms and lodge them with the Family Assistance Office or Centrelink. Don't delay as you may not be able to backdate payments.

If you are claiming a Centrelink payment, you may also be able to register an Intent to Claim by phone, in person or over the Internet. If you then lodge your claim form within a fortnight, payments may be backdated to the date you registered your intent. However, this may not be possible for the whole range of benefits on offer.

You might be required to attend an interview to determine your eligibility. Depending on what you are claiming, you may need to provide proof of your baby's birth, you and your partner's identity, age, residence, income/assets and your tax file number. Make sure you know which documents you need to take or time could be wasted in processing your claim.

Getting paid

The amount you receive depends on your financial circumstances. For an idea of what you may be entitled to, visit the Family Assistance Office or Centrelink website and click on 'online services'. The Family Assistance Estimator helps you work out how much you may get, and how your payments can alter if there's a change in your circumstances.

Change in circumstances

You need to notify the Family Assistance Office or Centrelink if you or your partner's circumstances change. Let them know if:

- you move;
- there is a change to your income or assets;
- you marry, divorce, separate, enter into a de facto relationship;
- you have or adopt a child;
- a child is no longer dependent on you; or
- there's a change to your residency status or you go overseas.

Otherwise, you might find yourself having to repay some or all of your payment.

If you disagree with a decision

If you think a decision is wrong you can ask for it to be reviewed. Try the following:

1. Contact the person who originally made the decision. Maybe there was a misunderstanding. Or maybe you can present new evidence to have the decision changed.
2. If this doesn't work, ask to have an Authorised Review Officer review the decision. This person wasn't involved in the original decision. He or she can change the decision if they agree it's wrong.
3. Still no luck? You can try appealing to the Social Security Appeals Tribunal. This is an independent body with the power to change decisions. Appealing is free. The hearing is informal, and many people choose to represent themselves. A friend or social worker can help if desired.
4. Your last port of call is the Administrative Appeals Tribunal. Appeals must be made within 28 days of the Social Security Appeals Tribunal's decision.

Maybe your problem is different. If you're unhappy with the way you've been treated, discuss the issue with a Customer Relations staff member. If this doesn't provide satisfaction and you want to take the matter further, you can make a complaint to the Commonwealth Ombudsman.

Keep in mind that under the Freedom of Information Act you have the right to inspect or obtain copies of your file. You generally cannot view information relating to others as the law protects such documents.

RISK OF OVERPAYMENT

Many families have been hit with debts arising from over-payment of government benefits. Paying it back isn't always easy. It might be recovered from your tax refunds or held back from future payments.

But how does this problem arise?

You need to estimate your income to receive FTB fortnightly or CCB as reduced fees. Then after the end of the financial year the Family Assistance Office calculates your exact entitlement using your actual income, in a process known as reconciliation.

So if your income turns out to be higher than you estimated, you've been overpaid and have to pay back the excess.

If your family income is between the FTB maximum rate ($31 755) and the cut-in point for the base rate and you earn $1000 more than you estimated, you've been overpaid by $300. So you can see the sum can get quite high if you're out by a few thousand.

Payment options

In early 2003, the federal government released its 'More choices for families' measure, increasing payment options and reducing the risk of overpayment. These choices are aimed at people who get their FTB as fortnightly payments or their CCB as reduced childcare fees.

If you or your partner's income increases, contact the Family Assistance Office and change your income estimate. You will receive a new rate. Some may still have been overpaid, however, and you can ask to have your remaining assistance adjusted for the rest of the financial year to recover or reduce that amount.

Another option is to claim FTB after the end of the financial year, either as a lump sum through the Family Assistance Office or through your tax return. Similarly, you can pay full childcare fees and later claim CCB as a lump sum through the Family Assistance Office (but not the ATO). Not everyone can afford to do this, however. Compromise measures are possible.

If you have trouble estimating your income—say because you are self-employed or a casual worker—you can receive the base rate of FTB fortnightly (or minimum rate of CCB) and claim the rest after the end of the financial year. If you are a single income family and one of you plans to go back to work, you can leave your FTB Part B until after the end of the financial year while still receiving Part A fortnightly. And if you have a child who you expect to start working, you can defer any payment for that particular child while still being paid for younger children.

That way, you reduce the risk of being overpaid. After the end of the financial year, the Family Assistance Office will check what your family's actual income was and work out if you are owed any extra money.

Coming up with compromises

Jackie is an at-home mother of two. She and her husband Bob receive FTB Parts A and B and CCB as reduced fees for her oldest child. Next year things will change. Her oldest child will start school and her youngest will start attending long daycare.

Jackie has decided to go back to work on a casual basis next year and is unsure how much she will earn. It's very likely she'll lose her entitlement to FTB Part B. She'll probably earn enough to reduce their FTB Part A entitlement but not enough to lose it completely.

To reduce the risk of overpayment, Jackie and Bob decide to claim only the base rate of FTB Part A fortnightly. Then after the end of the financial year, they'll be paid the remainder of their entitlement—if any—as a lump sum.

They've also decided to get the minimum rate of CCB as reduced fees, and be paid any remainder after the end of the financial year.

This way they are at least receiving some assistance, while reducing the possibility of having to pay back hundreds of dollars (or more) further down the track.

FURTHER HELP

- Family Assistance Office and Centrelink—for information about eligibility, rates etc. call 136 150. See also http://www.centrelink.gov.au and http://www.familyassist.gov.au.
- Australian Taxation Office—for information on the Baby Bonus and claiming Family Tax Benefit through the tax system call 132 861 and see http://www.ato.gov.au.

- Commonwealth Ombudsman—if you are unhappy with the way you have been treated by a government body, call 1300 362 072.
- Social Security Appeals Tribunal—1800 011 140.

Useful publications

Centrelink, July 2003, 'Are you a parent or guardian? A guide to your options and our services', Centrelink.

Family Assistance Office, July 2003, 'More choices for families—reduce the risk of being overpaid', Centrelink.

Family Assistance Office, July 2003, 'Your guide to family assistance', Centrelink.

Part 3

As they grow

11

Educating your child

A decent education is a must for any child and in an ideal world it wouldn't cost the earth. But it can be one of the major expenses parents face, particularly if they choose private rather than public schooling. Whatever your choice, however, there are ways to reduce costs without jeopardising your child's learning experience. In this chapter we look at typical costs, ways to cut those costs, potential sources of financial assistance, and saving for education strategies.

Note that this chapter focuses on the costs of primary and secondary school only. Government policies for university and other tertiary institutions are always changing. From the days of full fees, to the days of no fees, to the current Higher Education Contribution Scheme (HECS) (which is even now undergoing significant reforms), who knows what the system will be by the time your child grows up and gets there? As circumstances change so much and tertiary education is still a long way off, there's not much point going into it.

Something else that *is* relevant, however, is the cost of all those extracurricular activities that school aged children enjoy. Sports, dancing, music and so forth. What sorts of prices can you expect to pay? And again, how can you keep these costs down to a reasonable level?

COSTS OF SCHOOLING

How much does it cost to send your child to school? The answer depends primarily on whether you select private or public schooling. Some people insist that the more costly an education, the better it is. Not everyone agrees with that, but all parents want their children to have the best education possible.

The choice between public and private education comes down to many things—your budget, your expectations, your religious stance and your own schooling experience. Money isn't always the primary factor in your choice, but the difference in cost is tremendous.

It's not just school fees. There are many additional costs. These vary between schools, and tend to be higher at private schools where you are expected to buy more of your own textbooks and equipment. Private schools also tend to have excursions that are more expensive and costly extracurricular activities may be the norm. Similarly, public schools in affluent areas tend to have higher ancillary costs than their more moderate counterparts. This chapter looks at all of the costs that you may encounter, before going on to suggest some ways to trim those costs.

School fees—public versus private

If you select a private school you can expect to pay significant fees. Fees are several thousand dollars per year, some marked in the tens of thousands. Enough to make most of us break into a sweat. If you want your child to board at the school, it will be even more costly. Keep in mind that private school fees vary markedly and you need to compare these as well as other issues (such as reputation, areas of excellence, travel) when you make your choice. The difference in price can be as high as tens of thousands of dollars from start to finish.

Usually you need to book your child in many years in advance, possibly while they are still infants. You may be asked to pay a sum when you register as an indication of your good faith. Chances are this is non-refundable if you later decide not to enrol in the school. Many private schools also charge an entrance fee that can be a few hundred or even a few thousand in itself.

Catholic schools generally cost less than other private schools but fees can still run into the low thousands per year. You do not need to be Catholic to send your child there; some places are usually offered to non-Catholic Christians.

Government schools are by far the cheapest. Depending on the state you live in you may be asked to make a small and/or voluntary contribution to school fees. But you may not have much say in which government school your child will attend. The school you are zoned for must take you on, but if you want to enrol in a non-local school it may be difficult. Depending on state laws, you may need to demonstrate a valid reason why your child should attend an out-of-area school. Contact the school of your choice and ask them for enrolment application details.

Bond

Private schools may require a bond prior to entry. It is repaid when your child leaves the school on condition that all monies owing have been paid, all books returned and so forth.

Building funds

Private and Catholic schools may levy an extra charge to help pay for building and grounds' maintenance.

Uniforms

A major expense, considering the rate at which children grow. You need to purchase winter and summer standard uniforms as well as winter and summer sports uniforms. Include a hat or cap, school shoes, sports shoes, and a school bag to provide the minimum requirements. Depending on the school and the rate at which your child grows and wears out clothes, you could be paying anywhere between $200 and $2000 per year for uniforms. Why such a huge range? Private school uniforms tend to cost far more than public school uniforms. And even the costs of public school uniforms vary depending on the school's policy and how strictly uniform codes are adhered to.

Textbooks

Costs are quite low in public schools, particularly in the early years. During the first few years you may be up for less than $50, as most resources are provided by the school itself. In private schools, however, you are usually expected to buy a lot more.

Stationery

Pens, pencils, pencil cases, erasers, rulers, maths sets, exercise books, and so forth. They add up and need replacing often.

Lunches

Something we tend to forget when working out the costs of schooling. Allow for the costs of canteen food or for providing packed lunches yourself.

Travel

If you drive your children to school allow for the additional costs of petrol.

Excursions

Excursions are considered an essential component of the school curriculum, rather than mere entertainment. Costs depend on locations and activities but schools usually pay discounted fares and entry fees. When it comes to camps and retreats the costs start to rise.

Sports equipment

This can become pricey, depending on the sports your child participates in. Public schools may foot the bill but private schools might not. If this is an area of special interest for your child it is worth raising the issue with the school.

Private tutoring

Not compulsory as far as the schools are concerned, but many parents want their children to have a private tutor. Tutoring can be provided by coaching colleges or privately. An average sort of price is $30 per hour lesson but rates do vary markedly.

TRIMMING THE COSTS

Take heart. There are many ways to cut the costs of your child's education without necessarily sacrificing quality. Re-examining the above categories, you might be able to save money in the following ways:

Fees

If you want to enrol your child in a private or Catholic school, ask the school about scholarships. Scholarships allow for some remission of tuition fees. They can be awarded on various bases, such as academic, sporting or musical ability. Your financial circumstances might be taken into account.

Uniforms

Uniforms may be available both at the school and at uniform specialist stores. Compare prices. Schools also often provide secondhand uniforms at a fraction of the price. Some can be in very good condition but it's best to get in early.

A great deal also depends on how strict the school is. Simply wearing the school colours satisfies some schools. So for the winter uniform, for instance, rather than purchasing a relatively costly girls' tunic, your daughter might be able simply to wear a track suit and skivvy of the appropriate colours—which can be purchased at inexpensive general stores. Check this with the school first, of course. Younger siblings can benefit from hand-me-down uniforms and shoes.

Textbooks

A particular source of strain for private secondary students. Students might be able to save by buying secondhand texts. Many also survive simply by using the library.

Lunches

While school canteens are generally good value, you can still save by making packed lunches. It's a matter of weighing up your time and the cost saving. Discourage too much reliance on the canteen for snack foods—one way to do this is to tell young children that they have to pay for snacks out of their own pocket money. As well as saving money you may also be protecting your child from long-term health problems. Many schools allow unhealthy and non-nutritious foods to be sold in their canteens, and this is now a recognised factor in the rapid rise in childhood obesity rates.

Travel

Check with the school about the availability of free or concession travel. Better still, walk your children to school if possible. It's good exercise and it's free.

Private tutoring

If your child needs one, shop around for a good value tutor. You can also cut costs by sharing tutors, perhaps with a friend or neighbour whose children are studying at the same level as your children.

WHAT MATTERS MOST

Remember, when it comes to education, nothing is more important than your child's enthusiasm and your moral support. Instilling a love of learning is more a matter of outlook than money. Take a personal interest in your child's education right from the outset, when attitudes to learning are being formed. A small investment of your time costs you nothing, but is the most valuable input into your child's education, both present and future.

COSTS OF SCHOOL HOLIDAYS

On average, school children have twelve weeks of holidays per year. Although a time relished by most children, for many parents it means extra bills.

Vacation care

If, like most people, you only get four weeks' annual leave, you may have to make arrangements for vacation care. Depending on the service, this can cost you $30 to $50 per day. Five days a week, eight weeks a year can amount to around $1200 to $2000.

If you and your partner are willing to take leave at different times, you can stretch your four weeks each to eight weeks all up.

Of course if you have friends or relatives who can lend a hand you can cut vacation care costs dramatically. Maybe your parents are willing and able to take on the task of minding your children, even if only for a day or two. It reduces the financial strain and gives your kids some time out. Or maybe you can share days with friends or a group of friends, particularly if you work on different days.

Striving for balance

Sharon and George both work full-time, with the standard four weeks' annual leave each. They have two children, both at school. Sharon and George want to minimise the time their children spend in vacation care, partly because of expense, partly because they want their kids to spend some time at home with family.

They decide to split up their leave, not taking it in blocks. George's mother agrees to take the kids one day a week during school holidays, and they book vacation care two days per week. That leaves two days per week to contend with, or at most 24 days all up (less when you consider some of these days are public holidays).

Their annual leave combined more than covers this period if they don't take it simultaneously. And there are enough days over so they can take some leave together, and go on an annual family holiday.

Holiday entertainment

The other issue that arises, whether you work or not, is how to keep children entertained during holidays. Do your kids say, 'I'm bored' first thing in the morning on day one? Do you wonder how you'll survive the next fortnight?

If you look back at Chapter 6, 'Ongoing costs' you will find a list of suggestions for general low cost leisure activities. Here I'd just like to add a few points relating specifically to school holidays:

- Kids' clubs. These are run during holidays by churches and community groups. Activities include craft and games, and morning or afternoon tea is often provided. They generally last a few hours a day, for a few days only. But they are great value (just a few dollars a day) and provide a welcome relief for parents and children alike.
- Library activities. Many public libraries have special craft/ story sessions during school holidays.
- Hobby classes. You might not be able to afford hobby classes on a weekly basis, but what about for a day or two over the holidays? Art and craft classes for children are often run during school holidays, and can cost around $20 to $40 per session, depending on the costs of materials and the duration of the class.
- Camps. Organised by schools, churches, sports associations and community groups. Prices depend on destination, accommodation, length of stay and so forth, but can be a couple of hundred dollars for a few days' stay.
- Family holidays. Here prices can vary from under a hundred dollars to thousands. At one end you have the humble camping or caravan holiday, where the main expenses may be petrol, food, camping permits and entrance fees to various attractions; at the other end of the spectrum you have the five star resorts. In the middle are the rented homes/apartments and the relatively modest motels or motor inns. Up to your inclination and budget.

GOVERNMENT FINANCIAL ASSISTANCE

Back to school allowance

All families with children enrolled in New South Wales schools (kindergarten to Year 12) are entitled to a back to school allowance. It is paid regardless of whether the child attends a public or private school. The allowance is $50 per child each year. The purpose of the allowance is to help meet the costs of school basics such as uniforms, shoes or books. At the time of writing New South Wales is the only state to provide this allowance.

General assistance for families

Many families are entitled to financial assistance from the federal government. Although not specifically designed for education, the payments can be used to help meet the costs of schooling. Chapter 10, 'Government assistance' looks at these payments in detail.

Talk to the principal

If you are having trouble paying public school fees or meeting the costs of books, talk to the principal. Depending on state laws, there may be a provision to waive fees or other assistance may be available.

Help for tertiary students

Earlier I stated it wasn't worth looking too closely at the situation of tertiary students as policies change and I'm assuming your children are still very young. But I will do one thing. I can point you in the right direction. If you want to know more about tertiary fees and HECS, refer to the website http://www.hecs.gov.au. For information about the upcoming reforms to student financing, see http://www.backingaustraliasfuture.gov.au run by the Commonwealth Department of Education, Science and Training.

EXTRACURRICULAR EXPENSES

Apart from the costs of actual schooling, you also need to factor in all the extracurricular activities that your child is likely to participate in. Be it swimming lessons, piano, ballet, soccer or gym, these after school activities all cost money. Some more than others.

Swimming lessons, for example, can cost around $10 per lesson. Sports such as soccer can cost about $150 per season, but you need to provide some or all of the gear. Learning an instrument can cost anywhere from $20 to $40 per half hour lesson—and of course you need to have the instrument as well.

Dance classes can also cost around the $10 per class mark, but there are many ancillary expenses. Costumes, shoes, music licensing fees, concert tickets, concert photographs and videos all add up at an alarming rate.

Gym classes can vary—I've come across ones that cost $60 per ten-week term and others that cost $250. Try ones run by community organisations for better value. Joining the Boy Scouts or Girl Guides is also relatively inexpensive.

This is an area where parents may need to make choices. Given the chance, many primary school aged children will gleefully take on nearly any task. Too many activities can over-burden children and put a strain on your finances. As a family, you need to choose which to focus on and which to let go, particularly as your child grows older and has more school work to contend with.

How to cut costs

As always, shop around. I'm not saying choose activities specif-ically because of their cost, but once you know what activity you are interested in, look around for the best value. Of course you will also need to consider matters such as reputation, prox-imity and compatibility, the latter being particularly important for long-term one-on-one activities such as music lessons. Word of mouth can help you with your decision, but you need to come to your own conclusion.

Once you make your choice, there are ways to save money on extracurricular activities. Consider:

- car pooling for travel to sporting events (training as well as competitions), saving on the costs of petrol;
- taking along your own snacks and refreshments to sporting venues, swimming pools and so on to avoid the costs of kiosks;

- buying secondhand costumes or using hand-me-downs for sports and dance classes and concerts;
- hiring a musical instrument as opposed to buying it outright. This may be more costly in the long run, but it may be worth it if you are unsure whether your child will stick to their lessons or not;
- buying secondhand music or other necessary instructional books;
- attending group music classes as opposed to private tuition. Keep in mind that the standard and rate of learning may be lower if you choose that option, but it may be a good way to start young children off and see if their interest develops.

Maybe you can go back to bartering. For instance, do you have an acquaintance who can teach your child an instrument? Would they be willing to give your child lessons in return for something else—for instance you could agree to pick up their children from school in the afternoons, or teach their children something in your line of expertise. Official organised lessons aren't the only way to learn and have fun.

SAVING FOR YOUR CHILD'S EDUCATION

Given how expensive it can be to educate your child, it's wise to work out an appropriate savings strategy. The sooner you start saving for your children's education, the better. As shown in Chapter 1, compounding makes a significant difference to the growth of your money and the effects are greater the longer the period invested.

Many parents select traditional savings and investment strategies. They might have a specific account, term deposit, life insurance policy or managed fund in their own names, earmarked for the child's educational needs. Or they might have a general pool that they draw upon as needed. Chapter 13, 'Securing your children's financial future' looks at investment options in more detail.

Education savings plans

But there are also specific education plans available, often offered by friendly societies. They involve regular investments into an education fund. The amount you deposit depends on when your child is due to start school and how much the education is likely to cost. There may be limits on the age your child can be on entry into the plan.

Money is paid out when the child reaches high school and/or (more commonly) tertiary studies, often as regular payments. But what happens if your child does not go on to tertiary education? What if they would rather have that money for something else, for instance to set up a business? Depending on the conditions of the fund, you may not lose your contributions but you might forfeit the earnings. Some allow you to nominate another child with an immediate family relationship who can take the benefit instead. Be sure you know exactly what the conditions are before you commit.

Changes to the law a few years ago mean that friendly societies have lost their tax exempt status. Income earned by friendly societies is now taxed at the company tax rate of 30 per cent. This is still attractive for parents who are on a higher marginal tax rate.

And there may be other tax advantages. Your child may have no tax liability during the education benefit accumulation stage—meaning they will not suffer the under-eighteen's staggering tax rates that apply to unearned children's income (see Chapter 13 for details). Furthermore, the fund might be able to claim a scholarships and bursaries tax offset at maturity, effectively reducing the tax paid out, and can then pass the benefit on to recipients.

If you are considering entering into an education savings plan, be sure to read the fine print. Make sure you know exactly what the tax benefits are, and weigh them up against the risk that your child will not continue on to tertiary education, thereby potentially losing the benefit accumulated. It is wise to consult a financial adviser before making an investment decision.

FURTHER HELP

- For more information on the costs of schooling and possible financial assistance, talk to the principal of the school in question. This is particularly so for private schools. For government school enquiries you can also contact your state's department of education.

12

Teaching kids to save

'I said no. Do you think I'm made of money? Put that back right now.'

We've all heard her, that frantic woman at the supermarket checkout. Trying desperately to prise the chocolate bar out of her toddler's iron grip while others in the queue click their tongues in disapproval.

Maybe you thought she handled it all wrong. Or maybe you winced and felt sorry for her. But did you ever expect to become her?

There's probably not one parent who hasn't had to struggle with their offspring snatching at the conveniently kid-height sweets. You can't blame the child, but it does highlight a rather important fact. Financial sense is not in-built. Like most things it has to be taught. But it's not as difficult as you might think.

DIFFERENT STAGES FOR DIFFERENT AGES

Once children are old enough not to shove coins straight into their mouths, they are old enough to start learning about money. Obviously the degree of understanding will relate to their age and level of maturity, and it's important to target your strategy to their particular stage. Expecting more of them just leads to frustration and—ultimately—spectacular supermarket tantrums.

TODDLERS

To a toddler, money is just another plaything with as much value as a button or a bean. They don't realise that money has a particular meaning any more than they can grasp the concept of compound interest. But this doesn't mean they shouldn't be exposed to it, under adult supervision of course.

A moneybox is a great idea for toddlers. It looks like a toy. They can spend many happy moments wrapping podgy little fingers around the coin and manoeuvring it into that little slot. Name the values as they insert them, explaining that the big ones are worth more than little ones. You might want to ignore $2 coins and notes for the moment; they just confuse matters. Once finished, your child will probably want to empty the money out and start all over again. Explain that the coins need to stay in the box until it's full, and then they can buy something with the money. Be specific. It helps if they can visualise the reward.

You might also want to ask grandparents and other doting visitors to give the child the odd coin or two for their moneybox rather than chocolates and lollies. Just a thought.

PRESCHOOLERS

Children aged three to five are becoming more social and confident. Next time you buy them a particular item, say a packet of biscuits, allow them to hand the money over to the sales assistant. Tell your child that the money is paying for that packet. If your child then asks for something else explain that the money was spent on the biscuits and cannot be spent on anything else. It won't be long before they make the link.

Similarly, when you visit the bank or pay a bill give your child a running commentary on what you are doing and why. Something like: 'We have to pay money to use our telephone. If we don't we can't ring people up anymore and no one can ring us.' Preschoolers see us handing over money in shops, but seldom realise that other things also need to be paid for.

PRIMARY SCHOOL CHILDREN

This is where it really begins. The earlier work was laying the foundation, now you need to build on it. All school-aged children know about pots of gold and pirate treasure, but don't yet appreciate that wealth is built, not found. Perhaps the best way to teach them is to let them have their own money, then guide how they handle it.

Pocket money—how deep should your pockets be?

Pocket money introduces children to the basics of budgeting. They learn how to handle a regular income and how to make it last until the next payday. Ideally they will spend a portion and save the rest for future larger purchases.

So the question is, how much? Many parents go for the rule of thumb '50 cents for each year of life', but this may not suit you. Before you decide ask yourself what you expect your child to do with the money. Do they need to buy their own snacks and/or school meals? Toys? Books? To a large degree this will be related to their age, but you need to be sure that your expectations are commensurate with the sum.

At what age should you start? Requests for pocket money usually begin when children discover the school canteen and see other children spending money. It's up to you to decide when your child is sufficiently mature to ration their money and not spend it all on lollies in one go.

As for how to give it to them, again, there is no hard and fast answer. It all depends on your parenting style. Only you can judge, and it might take a bit of experimentation and fine tuning before you are satisfied.

Still, it helps to know your options:

- Pay a regular sum each week with no strings attached.
- Pay a regular sum each week but only if the child meets set criteria, for example doing their homework and tidying their room.
- Pay for services rendered. Some families have complex tables drawn up: a certain sum for making their bed, a different amount for drying the dishes and so on. Or you might choose to make every task of equal value. Either way, the more the child works, the more they earn. Some families believe this

reflects the real world, others think it sends the message that the only reason to help out at home is money.

- Don't give them pocket money at all, but provide funds when particular items are requested. The merits of purchasing the item, particularly the cost, are then discussed on a case-by-case basis.

You might want to try a combination of the above. Consistency matters, but it is also important to build in sufficient flexibility to meet your child's changing maturity levels and financial needs.

Alex's allowance

Gina uses a combination of pocket money strategies. She gives eight-year-old Alex $4 per week on the condition that he makes his bed each morning and sets the dinner table each evening. He pays for his own school snacks. If he wants extra money he must carry out additional household duties. The amount he is paid for these is negotiable, and depends on what he wants to purchase and why. If the item is significantly out of his reach but Gina thinks he should have it, she may buy it for him as long as Alex contributes to the cost—even if only by a small fraction.

Keeping up with the Jones's

'But Emily gets much more than me. It's not fair. I never get anything.' Add a touch of attitude and you get the picture. Children are very aware of how much money their friends are receiving and can become quite distressed if they get less. In many schools it is a measure of status. So what do you do if you are not able—or indeed, not prepared—to match their friends' exorbitant allowance levels? And, on a bigger scale, how do you explain that you can't afford to go on holiday, buy a new bike, get them their own computer and so on?

Very young children may not understand that different parents have different incomes and assets. If they think about it at all, they assume that everyone has equal wealth. You need to explain the realities gently and with patience. Older primary school children are probably aware of it, but still find it hard to cope with the consequences. Like most parenting matters, you need to be firm but understanding. Make it clear that you decide what is right for your family, you do what you believe is best and that you are not out to make their life a misery.

Savings accounts

This is another great teaching method. Your children might not be thrilled initially—especially when pocket money and gifts abscond into their account—but as the balance grows a sense of achievement will gradually be awakened.

Very young children cannot have accounts in their own names. You can, however, open one in your name in trust for the child. Once they reach school age children can open savings accounts in their own names provided their parents operate the account. By age twelve they can withdraw money with their own signature. Once they reach their teens, you may feel they are responsible enough for an account with ATM access.

But in the meantime, how do you select a savings account for your child?

Like everything else, you need to shop around. Some financial institutions offer products directly aimed at children. For example St George Bank has Happy Dragon passbooks, and the Commonwealth Bank has Dollarmite accounts, which are offered through many schools. Both are attractively packaged and inviting. Most other financial institutions don't offer specific products but their normal transaction accounts may be suitable. Most don't charge account keeping fees when the account is for a child, but don't assume. Always check. There's a current tendency to charge fees for kids' accounts that have ATM access.

Make regular deposits into the account and take your child with you. It doesn't matter if the sums are small; it's creating the habit that matters. Allow your child to hand the money and deposit slip to the teller. Often tellers praise with kind words, stamps or balloons, adding to the excitement of the venture.

For the tax considerations relating to children's savings accounts see 'Chapter 13—Securing your children's financial future'. The discussion also examines whether children need tax file numbers.

Checklist—choosing children's savings accounts

Visit a few banks, building societies and credit unions. When shopping around ask the following questions:

* Do you have a specific product directly aimed at children?
* If not, are any of your standard products suitable?
* Do you charge account keeping fees?
* Is a minimum balance required?
* What is the interest rate, and do you offer bonus or reward interest?
* How do you make your accounts inviting to children?

Also, look around. It helps if the institution is not intimidating and dull.

* Are the queues short?
* Is the institution child friendly and appealing?
* Do the tellers have a rapport with children?

Doing the sums

Thirteen-year-old Sandra opened an account on her birthday with an initial balance of $10. The deal is bonus interest at the rate of 3 per cent per year if she makes at least one deposit and no withdrawals in a given month. As she is a child no monthly account keeping fees are charged. She goes on to save $10 a month and makes no withdrawals. On her eighteenth birthday she will have $646.47.

In working this out it was assumed that 3 per cent per annum equates to 0.0025 per cent per month. The final sum was calculated using a basic annuity calculation, which assumes a constant interest rate and regular equal deposits. In reality a child will probably go on to save more than $10 per month as he or she grows older, so the final balance may be significantly higher. The interest rate is also unlikely to remain constant over the course of so many years.

The benefit of compound interest—or earning interest on your interest—is explained in Chapter 1, 'Before you begin'.

TEENAGERS

With teenagers the emphasis should be on open and honest communication. Negotiation is the key.

Get them involved

It might feel odd to sit around the dinner table discussing family finances with your children, but give it a go. Remember you are not asking them to make the actual decisions (unless you'd rather have a new Nintendo than a dishwasher). Neither do you want to burden them with financial pressures. Rather the aim is to gradually expose them to the decision-making process.

Emphasise that finances are limited and choices need to be made. For instance the family might need to choose between adding a new room to the house and upgrading the car. Ask your children what they would do in your place. Hopefully they will gain an insight into the types of issues that determine the outcome. Not only will it teach them valuable financial lessons, it just might reduce family feuds as well.

The mobile phone issue

A question that never arose when we were kids but is now in the mind of nearly every parent: should their teenager have a mobile phone?

On the one hand there's the safety issue. If your child is stranded, lost or hurt, they can call for help. On the other hand there's the cost issue. It's very easy for costs to skyrocket: mobiles can be expensive toys. As most parents know, when teens talk to their friends, it can be hard to stop.

You may want to look upon the issue as a way of teaching your teenager financial responsibility. Using mobile phones wisely involves an ongoing commitment and an ability to keep to reasonable limits.

One option is to allow a mobile on a trial basis, ensuring your child won't use it recklessly. Of course if you are committed to a plan, you're still required to pay the ongoing costs for the duration of the plan. For older teenagers you might leave the whole responsibility to them, and expect them to pay for the phone out of their own money.

You can go for prepaid mobiles as a way to keep a lid on costs. However, you run the risk that your child won't be able to use the mobile in an emergency situation. With prepaids you need to consider the cost of the phone, the cost of the card (often $25–30, $50–60, and $100) and its access period (often two, six or twelve months) and the cost of recharging. You might agree to only pay for recharging at reasonable intervals.

What about plans? They vary from $10–20 per month (some even zero) to $150 plus. It's very hard to choose between the various carriers' plans as they are just different enough to prevent direct comparison. You need to consider free calls, flag falls, call costs, peak and off-peak rates, costs of the phone itself and network coverage. Not an easy task. Try visiting http://www.phonechoice.com.au, the website of an Australian company that provides free independent information on mobile phone costs.

Part-time jobs

Many teenagers enter the workforce, if only on a part-time basis while they continue studying. In today's competitive labour market this can be a definite bonus. But apart from that, part-time employment can help young people learn the value of money. Once they have truly worked for something, money and what it buys suddenly takes on a whole new meaning. And that is exactly what we want them to learn.

You may need to rethink your strategy once your child starts to work part-time. Chances are they will still not be financially independent. How will you handle requests for money for outings? For clothes? For textbooks and other educational materials?

You might decide to continue paying them an allowance to help make up any shortfalls. You might decide to help them out with particular purchases that you feel they ought to have, and require them to dip into their savings for luxuries. But what about major purchases, such as a car or a computer, where they haven't saved enough and you're not inclined to cough up the entire sum? One tried and true method is to match your child's savings dollar for dollar. This helps them meet their goals while still encouraging them to save as much as they can.

In any case it is always best to discuss your reasons with your child. Allow them to have their say and to express their own point of view.

Full-time jobs

Many children start full-time work long before they leave home. The issue of money now swings around and the question becomes—should they be paying you? If you decide you want (or indeed need) your child to contribute to the family's finances, discuss the various options with them. It's best if the arrangement is made jointly and suits you both. You might decide on:

- a regular sum for board;
- a contribution to various bills, such as electricity and gas;
- a separate phone service for your child, paid for by him or her;
- a contribution to cost of groceries; or
- a combination of the above.

AT ANY AGE—GO SOFTLY

Regardless of the age of your child, it's important to teach money sense with tact and understanding. Don't give them the impression that saving is a form of punishment. Be positive, and show them that saving leads to future rewards. It's why adults do it, after all.

FURTHER HELP

Useful publications

Koch, D. and Koch, L. 1995, *I'm Not Made of Money: A Parent's Guide to Teaching your Kids about Money*, Australian Financial Press, Sydney.

Koch, S. 2000, *The Teenager's Guide to Money*, Allen & Unwin, Sydney.

Whitcomb, J.E. 2002, *The Sink or Swim Money Program: A 6-step Plan for Teaching your Teenager Financial Responsibility*, Simon & Schuster, Sydney.

13

Securing your children's financial future

All families need some sort of investment strategy, well thought out and implemented. Whether you want to save for your children's education, buy them a car, help them with the deposit for a home, or just provide for a prosperous future—you need a plan. Simply coasting along year after year will get you nowhere, and before you know it, time will run out.

ASSETS IN KIDS' NAMES

Parents sometimes want to put assets into their children's names. The reasons vary. They might want to teach their children how to save. They might want to help the children financially, or they might think (wrongly) that they will be getting a major tax break.

The traditional approach is the savings account in the child's name. But as we become more financially sophisticated, we find parents putting shares in children's names or holding them in trust on behalf of their children.

Savings accounts for very young children should be opened in the parent's name as trustee for the child. It's only once kids reach school age that they can have accounts in their own names. Even then, the parents need to be signatories to the account until the child is old enough to take over, usually at age twelve.

Which leads us to an interesting question.

Who owns the money earned from these assets—the parent or the child? Or, more to the point, who declares the earnings for tax purposes?

There is no clear cut answer. The name that the account is in is not definitive. Instead, the key factor is who *uses* the funds of the particular account. If the parent provides the money and spends it as desired, the parent should include the interest on his or her tax return. But if the funds derive from the child's own sources (such as gifts, pocket money, payment for odd jobs etc.) and the child is the only one who uses the money, then it belongs to the child.

In whose interest?

Maddy is seven and attends school. She has an account in her own name, and her father is signatory to the account. The balance of her account is small, made of up money given to her by her relatives for birthdays and Christmas. She also makes small infrequent deposits of saved-up pocket money. The funds in the account belong to Maddy, and any interest earned is considered to be hers.

Brian opens an account for his three-year-old daughter. The account is in Brian's name, in trust. Brian deposits money into the account and only uses it to pay for his daughter's expenses—such as clothing, toys, preschool fees and presents. Although he spends the money on the child, he's the one who uses the account, so the money is considered to be his. He needs to declare the interest earned in his tax return.

TAX FILE NUMBERS (TFNs) FOR KIDS' ACCOUNTS

Do you need to quote a TFN for children's savings accounts? You're no doubt aware that you aren't legally required to quote a TFN for any account, but if you don't then withholding tax of 48.5 per cent will be deducted from the interest earned.

There is no age limit for a child to get a TFN. The main difference between the rules governing adults and children is in the size of the threshold that applies before tax is withheld. The threshold for adult's savings accounts is currently $120—if more is earned, tax is withheld.

The ATO has outlined the following rules for accounts held in children's sole names:

- Children under sixteen earning less than $420 in investment income per year do not need to quote a TFN, but must provide their date of birth.
- Children under sixteen earning over $420 in investment income should quote their TFN to prevent TFN withholding tax, as well as providing their date of birth.
- Children over sixteen who earn less than $120 in investment income per year don't need to quote a TFN.
- Children over sixteen earning over $120 in investment income need to quote their TFN to prevent withholding tax.

For accounts held by parents on behalf of the child, the parents should quote their (the parents') TFNs. If there is a formal trust, then the trust's TFN is to be quoted. For joint accounts between parent and child, the threshold amount is the adult threshold of $120.

Note that the thresholds apply per account, not per child. You can't put all your children's names on the account and expect the threshold to go up.

In the case of dividend income, the threshold is just $1 for both adults and children.

Do kids need to lodge tax returns?

If the child's only source of income is interest, and it is less than $643, a return does not need to be lodged. If TFN withholding tax applied, a return is needed to obtain a refund.

Tax on children's non-wage earnings

Say the money invested belongs to your child. They bear the tax liability on the earnings, not you. Does this mean you can reduce your family's overall tax bill by placing assets in your children's names? Surely they'll have a low marginal tax rate?

Sorry, but that's not so.

Children's non-wage income is taxed at incredibly steep rates. Let me emphasise the *non-wage* bit. Children's income derived from employment and inheritance is taxed at ordinary rates.

But as for interest, dividends, and family trust distributions children can only earn up to $416 per year tax free. If this were their only source of income, they would qualify for the low income tax offset so the threshold goes up to $643. Once they creep over, children earning between $417 and $1445 are taxed at a staggering 66 per cent of the sum in excess of the threshold. Once over $1445, the rate drops down to a flat 47 per cent, the highest marginal tax rate. Adequate disincentive to placing significant assets in your kids' names, wouldn't you say?

FAMILY TRUSTS

This is not a type of investment, rather a way of holding investments. A trust is an agreement that binds a person or body (known as the trustee) to hold property on behalf of others (the beneficiaries) for the others' benefit. The document creating the trust is known as the trust deed.

Family trusts are created to benefit particular members of a family. They allow parents to make provision for their children's future, particularly those that are too young to own property in their own names. And some parents may want their adult offspring to have the benefit of family wealth, but not total control over the assets.

There are two types of family trusts:

- discretionary trusts, where the trustee decides which of the beneficiaries gets income and capital from the trust; and
- non-discretionary trusts, where the trustee does not get to choose, but must follow what is stipulated in the deed.

Most family trusts are discretionary. Why? Because the trustee can direct income to family members on low tax rates. Discretionary trusts can also be flexible and respond to changing needs, for instance if a beneficiary has a baby and wants to stop work for a while, or if another is going through a divorce. It wouldn't be attractive to distribute too much income to a minor because, as we saw above, children's non-wage earnings are taxed at prohibitively high rates.

A few years back there were proposals to tax family trusts as companies, but this was put on hold and to date has still not happened.

It must be said that the tax issues relating to trusts are very complicated. Trusts themselves are expensive to set up and maintain, and are not a viable concern for many of us. If you are considering setting up a family trust, be sure to seek legal and financial advice.

Things change, and what is good today may not be good for the future. Ensure the trust has the flexibility to meet future needs.

Setting up a trust in your will to provide for under-aged children is a different matter. This is known as a testamentary trust. For more information, see Chapter 15, 'Beyond your lifetime'.

INVESTMENT CONSIDERATIONS

When it comes to investing for your family's future, what sorts of things do you need to consider?

Your investment personality

Just as investments vary, so do investors. Before you commit yourself and your money, it is important to understand your investor profile. There's no point entering high risk markets if the stress will keep you awake at nights. Similarly, if you know little about investing and have no time to track market fluctuations, direct investments in shares may not be for you.

So what type of investor are you? The answer depends partly on your personality, partly on your life stage. You might be conservative by nature, or you might be more adventurous and enjoy taking risks. And if you're saving up to start a family you might be putting your energy into short-term savings strategies, while if you've just had a baby, you might be struggling to adjust to your new situation. As your children grow, you may be looking to invest for the future. That's not to say you should procrastinate. Don't use your stage of life as an excuse to put off determining the strategy that best suits your needs. The sooner you work out an effective strategy, the greater the benefit will be.

Your investment timeframe

Your timeframe affects the type of investments you select. It varies depending on whether you have children yet and if so, how old they are. It depends on when you want to have access to the funds.

Ask yourself what you want to do with your money. Buy a new family car? Save for your children's education? Plan for your retirement? All of the above?

It all boils down to your financial goals.

If you haven't done so already, sit down with a pen and paper. List your goals and when you want them achieved. Anything under two to three years is short-term. Long-term we're looking at five to ten years or more. Work out your order of priority—not just in terms of timing, but also in terms of importance. Only then can you start to consider what type of investments would best suit you.

Risk versus return

There's a general rule of thumb when it comes to investing: the higher the potential return, the higher the risk faced.

This is where your timeframe comes in. Conventional wisdom is to keep risks low for short-term goals. Cash is typically regarded as low risk and low return, but everyone needs a certain amount of cash for daily living expenses. Fixed interest securities, such as fixed term deposits and government bonds, offer a fixed interest rate over a fixed period. The longer the term, the higher the return. Returns are relatively low in today's low inflation environment.

Once you have enough cash, consider something more adventurous for the long-term. You may already have a direct property interest in your own home. Do you want to invest in property beyond that—either directly or by way of a property trust? How about shares? Shares historically have some of the highest returns, but market volatility and uncertainties also make them significantly more risky than conservative cash investments. In the long run, however, fluctuations tend to iron out and the general trend is often up. There's no guarantee in any given case, of course, but if you invest over the long-term and diversify over a good spread of markets, generally the risks become more acceptable.

Diversifying means not 'putting all your eggs in one basket'. If one investment does not perform as well as expected at any given time, the performance of another might make up for it. Professional advice should be sought.

The risks of inflation

If you consider yourself risk averse, here's something to chew over. Many finance experts claim that the real risk is not what happens in the markets in one month or one day. The real risk arises in falling behind inflation, which, in low return investments, eats away at your money over time. Not only can it reduce your 'real' (or inflation adjusted) interest, it can also chip into your principal.

Say your bank account pays 3 per cent interest. Ignore fees for the moment. If the inflation rate is 2 per cent, you are earning just 1 per cent in real terms. If inflation is 3 per cent, you aren't earning interest at all in real terms. If it's greater than 3 per cent, you're going backwards. When looking at investment figures keep inflation in mind and look at real returns, not just the nominal figures.

Income versus capital growth

Equally important is the question of what you want out of your investments. Do you want a steady income stream? Or are you prepared to forgo current earnings in order to grow your investment for the future? In other words, are you after capital growth?

In general, people approaching retirement might prefer investments that provide a regular income, such as cash and fixed interest. Younger people currently earning an income might prefer capital growth investments such as property and shares. They have time to be more aggressive with their investment strategy. Things are not quite so black and white, of course, as some shares skew towards providing income and some towards growth. It's an area you need to look into.

Direct investing versus managed funds

This is where your degree of knowledge becomes a real issue. Do you have the time and skills to select shares wisely, and then continue to monitor and analyse their performance? If you can answer yes, then go for it.

When it comes to selecting a stockbroker (someone who buys and sells shares on your behalf), you can choose between a discount broker and a full service broker. Full service brokers offer expert advice on your portfolio and make share recommendations. Discount brokers generally do not, so they tend to be cheaper. Internet brokers are becoming increasingly popular, and are relatively inexpensive.

Young parents in particular face time restrictions due to the need to balance career, home and family. If you don't have the time or expertise to manage your own investments, give some thought to buying into a managed fund.

Managed funds work by pooling together funds from many investors, allowing access to the sorts of markets that would otherwise be out of the reach of small investors. They can provide a portfolio far more diversified than a direct investor can generally afford.

Many charge entry, exit and management fees, and these should be factored in when making your choice. The Australian Securities and Investment Commission (ASIC) has a calculator on its consumer website (http://www.fido.asic.gov.au) that can estimate the fees you'll pay and the effect on your returns. The calculator only works if you want to invest a single lump sum, it won't work for additional regular contributions.

There is a wide range of funds that invest in different types of markets. Sifting your way through them is no easy task. Sure, once you select a fund you have professionals making those all-important decisions. But how do you pick the right one in the first place? Look back at your investor profile and remind yourself of your goals and priorities. Do as much research as you can, read as many product disclosure statements as possible. Keep in mind that past performance is no guarantee of future earnings. And seriously consider using the services of an investment adviser or financial planner.

Tax considerations

Is reducing your tax bill a motivating factor for investing? If so, you need to be aware of tax advantages when selecting your investments. Keep in mind that while tax is an important consideration, it should not be the sole basis for making investment decisions. Consider all aspects of an investment before committing yourself. Remember, your overall aim should be wealth maximisation, which isn't necessarily the same as tax minimisation.

Not all investments carry tax benefits. Investing in savings accounts and term deposits has no tax advantage. You pay full income tax on the interest you earn. And don't forget the impact of capital gains tax, which may apply when you dispose of an asset. Tax matters are complex, so always seek professional advice.

Dividend imputation

Australian shares carry the tax advantage of dividend imputation. This works by reducing an investor's tax liability by an amount known as the franking or imputation credit. Fully franked dividends are franked at the company tax rate: currently 30 per cent. While you still pay tax on the dividends, you receive a credit on the tax already paid by the company. This can be particularly attractive to investors whose marginal tax rate is below 30 per cent as the credit can be used to offset other tax payable. Low income and non-working spouses often have low marginal tax rates, and can take advantage of income splitting (where income earning assets are placed in the low earner's name).

Speaking frankly

It's easier to understand dividend imputation with an example. (For the sake of simplicity, we're ignoring the effect of the Medicare levy.)

Ron holds shares in an Australian company and receives $500 in franked dividends. The dividend is fully franked, meaning the company paid full tax at the company tax rate, which is 30 per cent.

When tax time comes around, Ron or his tax professional will need to add back the company tax to the value of the dividend. Known as grossing up, this will give us the pre tax worth of the dividend. Doing the sums,

$$
\begin{aligned}
\text{Imputation credit} &= 30/(100-30) \times \text{amount of dividend} \\
&= 0.43 \times 500 \\
&= \$215 \\
\text{Pre tax worth of dividend} &= \text{dividend} + \text{imputation credit} \\
&= 500 + 215 \\
&= \$715
\end{aligned}
$$

This $715 will be taxed at Ron's marginal tax rate. Say it's also 30 per cent. He would have been required to pay tax of $215 on the dividend, but as it's fully franked, he can use the $215 imputation credit. So in effect, the tax he pays on the dividend is zero.

If Ron had a marginal tax rate higher than the company tax rate, he would still have to pay some tax, but the amount would be reduced by the imputation credit. If his marginal tax rate were lower than 30 per cent, the excess would be offset against other tax liabilities.

Gearing

Gearing refers to borrowing money to invest. Negative gearing arises when the interest paid is higher than the asset's earnings. Generally, if there's a well founded expectation that the investment will produce income in excess of deductions within a reasonable timeframe, the interest paid may be tax deductible. As a tax strategy, negative gearing has its risks. There's always the possibility that the tax claim might be refused. Furthermore, the value of the investment might fall, leading to capital loss. Before embarking on any geared investment program, seek professional advice.

SUPER FOR YOUR CHILDREN?

Mostly when we think about providing for our children's future, we think in terms of helping them get a good start in life, then leaving something behind in our wills. But as of July 2002, a new consideration has arisen for parents. How do you feel about saving for—not just your own retirement—but for your children's?

It's possible with the introduction of child superannuation accounts.

It does seem an impossibly long way off, but due to the effect of compounding, the sooner you start investing, the faster the money will grow.

Consider the following example. If you invest $1000 now in a super fund that earns a net 7 per cent, after 40 years it would be worth $14 974. After 60 years it would be worth $57 946. A staggering difference. (The formula used for compounding is outlined in Chapter 1.) This is in today's dollars, however, and the real value will be much lower by then. Nevertheless, it illustrates the benefits of starting to save as early as possible.

And in the meantime, you are helping your children learn about the need to provide for the future. By the time they start earning an income they may have already developed some good attitudes towards investing.

How does it work?

Anyone can open a super account for a child. Parents, grandparents, family friends, whoever. But it must be done with the written consent of the child's parent, guardian, or legal personal representative.

You need to find a super fund that is prepared to accept child members. To date, there has been no active public marketing in this area, and you may need to search around.

Contributions on behalf of a child can be made up to a limit of $3000 per child in a three-year period. The fund trustee cannot accept more than that. (This limit doesn't apply to employer contributions for working children.) If you wish to contribute more than $3000 per three-year period, you will need to open another superannuation fund account. Although it sounds odd, the tax office states that no restrictions exist on the number of super accounts a child can have.

The child does not need to provide a tax file number to open an account.

The law requires that the child's parent, guardian or personal legal representative must make decisions in relation to the account. But once the child reaches sixteen, if desired you can notify the fund that your child will take over responsibility. Then they will make their own decisions. You may want to consider this if your child is working by then and receiving employer contributions. By age eighteen, of course, they're no longer legally children.

Tax implications

The contributions are not tax deductible to either the contributor or the child. However, super funds only pay tax at 15 per cent. Compare this to the tax rate on income earned on assets held in your kids' names in the more traditional manner. As we saw at the start of the chapter, such assets are slugged at a steep tax rate.

So it comes down to a trade off between tax considerations and the fact that super money is locked away for a very long time.

Is early access possible?

As with all super accounts, the benefits usually cannot be accessed until retirement. But early release may be possible in extremely limited circumstances if the child:

- is suffering severe financial hardship, meaning they cannot meet reasonable and immediate living expenses and they satisfy requirements regarding government income support; and/or
- qualifies under compassionate grounds: information on the categories of grounds and the relevant criteria can be

obtained from the Australian Prudential Regulation Authority (APRA) on 1300 131 060.

FURTHER HELP

- Australian Securities and Investment Commissions (ASIC) provides information about investment basics and finance professionals. Call the ASIC Infoline on 1300 300 630 or visit their consumer's website for financial tips and safety checks at http://www.fido.asic.gov.au.
- Australian Taxation Office—for information on the tax treatment of various types of investments and investment strategies, call 132 861 or visit their website at http://www.ato.gov.au.
- For help finding a financial adviser you can call the Financial Planning Association on 1800 626 393 or visit http://www.fpa.asn.au.

Useful publications

Australian Securities and Investment Commission and the Financial Planning Association 2002, 'Don't kiss your money goodbye. How to choose your financial planner and check your financial plan', revised edn, Australian Securities and Investments Commission and the Financial Planning Association of Australia.

Beelaerts, C. and Forde, K. 2003, *An Australian Investor's Guide to Stock Market, Property and Cash-based Investments*, 4th edn, Wrightbooks, Melbourne.

Clitheroe, P. 2002, *Managed Funds—How to Make Investing Easy*, Penguin Books, Melbourne.

Renton, N.E., 1997, *Family Trusts: A Plain English Guide for Australian Families of Average Means*, Wrightbooks, Melbourne.

Whittaker, N. 2001, *Shares Made Simple*, revised edn, Pan Macmillan, Sydney.

There are many more excellent books on investing—both general and specialist.

Part 4

Securing their futures

14

Coping as a single parent

Raising children on your own is an awesome prospect. It can be hard not having someone there to share ideas with and share the many responsibilities of parenthood. But life doesn't always go according to plan and sometimes we have no choice but to go it alone. A relationship might fail or your partner might die.

On top of all the other pressures that you may experience there is one that can't be thrust aside. How will you cope financially?

BREAKING UP

You've heard the statistics. Nearly half of all marriages end in divorce. Evidence shows that women suffer the most financially when a relationship breaks down, and this is particularly the case for mothers with young children. They face a double disadvantage—the high costs of raising children coupled with a reduced ability to earn a decent income.

Thankfully help is available. If you are already eligible for government assistance, the amount you are entitled to may rise if your relationship ends. If you don't currently receive a payment, you may now be eligible. See Chapter 10, 'Government assistance' for a detailed look at government benefits and contact Centrelink or the Family Assistance Office to discuss your particular situation.

PROTECTING YOUR FINANCIAL INTERESTS

There are some practical ways you can protect your interests. Do you and your partner have money in joint accounts? It's best to set up joint accounts so that both of you need to sign to withdraw the funds. If you can withdraw money on only one signature there's a danger your ex will empty the account. If it's too late there may well be legal redress further down the track, but in practical terms it's not always easy to get money out of someone once it's been spent.

You also want to prevent your ex running up debts that you may be liable for. Can your mortgage be increased without the need for both signatures? As with the joint account situation, this is best addressed at the outset, before the relationship sours. Do you have a credit card? If you are the principal cardholder and your ex is an additional cardholder, you are the one responsible for repayment. Consider cancelling the additional card.

And what about real property? If it's in both of your names, one can't sell it without the other. If your family home or investment property is in your partner's sole name, talk to a lawyer about seeking a court order from the Family Court. Known as a temporary or interlocutory injunction, the order restrains the other party from dealing with the property until further order of the court.

Make sure you write a new will. Depending on your state's laws divorce may not automatically revoke your will, meaning that any gift to your ex might still stand. If you have no will, property passes according to a strict legal formula and spouses rank number one. Make your new intentions clear by writing a will.

PROPERTY SETTLEMENTS

Twelve months after separation either partner can apply for a divorce. The actual divorce process is separate from the property settlement, which determines who gets what. You don't need to wait until the divorce before you sort out property matters—they are best addressed soon after the separation. In fact, if you haven't made suitable arrangements, one party will be required to commence proceedings for property orders within twelve months of the decree absolute (the final divorce decree).

The best approach to property settlements is calm discussion with an eye to coming to an agreement that satisfies you both.

Mediation services can help with this process—for information on their availability contact a lawyer or ask the Family Court. If you can come to an agreement, you can get a lawyer to draw it up and then have it formalised by the Court.

Things don't always run so smoothly, however. If you and your partner can't agree on a fair property division, you can ask the Family Court or the Federal Magistrates Court for an order. Try to find a lawyer with the necessary expertise. You can contact your state's Law Society (Law Institute in Victoria) for details regarding solicitors in your area. When you go to see your lawyer you will need to take information about your finances and your partner's finances: see the checklist below.

A property settlement covers all the property owned by the couple. This can include:

- your home and belongings;
- money;
- investment properties;
- shares, bonds and other investments;
- items that have been inherited;
- gifts;
- superannuation; and
- the family business.

It doesn't matter whose name the assets are in. Courts will consider the contribution of each partner. Contributions can be both financial and non-financial, such as child rearing and home making.

Your future financial needs will also be considered. Generally, the person who has the children living with them has the greater needs. Age, health and ability to earn an income are also considered.

What's the situation if you entered into a pre-nuptial agreement? In the past, these agreements were not enforceable, but the Court might have taken them into account as evidence of what would be a fair settlement in the circumstances. Since December 2000 it has been possible to make these agreements legally binding if independent legal and financial advice had been sought. More correctly known as financial agreements, they can be made before, during or after a marriage. Financial agreements can deal with property divisions and/or spousal maintenance.

Laws governing the property split of de facto couples vary between states. Generally it matters who paid for what, and future financial needs might not be taken into account. In some states, however, laws exist that provide rights more closely resembling those of divorcing couples.

Property settlements and/or maintenance orders can take a long time to come through, especially if there's a dispute. For help in the meantime it may be worth seeking legal advice concerning urgent or interim (temporary) orders. Contact Legal Aid to see if you are entitled to free legal assistance.

Checklist—What to take to your lawyer

When seeing a lawyer about a property settlement, try to take the following with you:

- your latest tax returns and assessments;
- pay slips;
- statements of bank, building society or credit union accounts;
- details of property ownership;
- details of debts such as home loans, personal loans;
- details of children's expenses such as school fees, childcare costs etc.;
- superannuation details;
- financial agreement, if relevant; and
- any other documents that reflect your financial position.

CHILD SUPPORT

Your financial responsibilities to your children survive the end of your relationship. Be it a divorce or the end of a de facto relationship, if you have children your duties continue. Never even lived together? It doesn't matter. Once paternity is established a duty arises to provide financial support.

But how is child support calculated and how is it paid?

The late 1980s saw the introduction of the Child Support

Scheme. Low payment levels and high default rates formed the impetus for the new system, which has made it considerably harder for payers to avoid coughing up. Because of these legislative changes two different child support systems now exist, known as Stage 1 and Stage 2. The one that applies to you is determined by a date.

Before 1 October 1989 (Stage 1)

If you separated before 1 October 1989 and all your children were born before that date, you come under the old system. The Family Court, Federal Magistrates Court, or Local/ Magistrates Court (the name of the latter varies between states) determines your application. You can come up with your own child support agreement and ask the Court to make consent orders, making your agreement enforceable. If you cannot come to an agreement that satisfies both of you the Court may have to decide the matter.

When making an order the Court will consider:

- each parent's income;
- the children's needs;
- the children's income and financial resources; and
- whether children from another relationship are being supported.

If you have a court order or court registered agreement under the old system, you can now ask the Child Support Agency (see below) to collect the payments on your behalf. The Agency can take the money directly from the payer's wage before he or she receives it, making it much more likely that it will be paid.

On or after 1 October 1989 (Stage 2)

If you separated on or after 1 October 1989 or one of your children was born on or after that date, you come under the new system. The Child Support Agency (an administrative body) has taken over the Court's role.

When it comes to working out child support under the new system you have various options. You can:

- Come to your own agreement as to the amount of support and how it will be paid, completely by-passing the Agency. You must be receiving either only the base rate of Family Tax Benefit or none at all. This option works best when the break up is amicable and you and your partner trust each other to work in the children's best interests.
- Come to your own agreement and lodge it with the Agency. You can arrange for collections to be made privately or ask the Agency to collect it on the payee's behalf. The Agency cannot draw up the agreement for you, but can provide information on mediation services that can help you reach a satisfactory solution. It's a good idea to seek legal advice when drawing up the agreement.
- Ask the Agency to determine the sum payable. Unlike the old system this doesn't require a court battle, but rather the application of an administrative formula. The formula takes into account the number of children that support is payable for, as well as both parents' income. The basic formula is modified in various situations, for instance where the payer has a high income (over $119 470 in 2003) or care is divided between both parents. Again, the sum can be paid directly or via the Agency.

The Child Support Agency website provides a handy online calculator that allows you to estimate the amount of support payable under the formula. Give it a go even if you prefer to reach your own agreement, as it provides an idea of what the entitlement would have been. Keep in mind that you need to know your partner's income before you can make use of the calculator. See http://www.csa.gov.au.

What if you choose the assessment option and you're unhappy with the result? Maybe special circumstances exist in your particular situation. For instance there may be high costs involved in contact with the children or maybe the child has special needs giving rise to extra costs. Either parent may be able to apply to the Child Support Agency for a change of assessment. If you're still not happy, seek legal advice.

Be sure to notify the Child Support Agency if your circumstances change. For instance if there's a change in care arrangements, employment or income levels. Also let them know if you and your partner reconcile or you settle down with a new partner.

Using the formula

After ten years of marriage Jonathon and Sarah decided to call it quits. Sarah took on major care of both their children, aged seven and five, and as such was entitled to child support. In 2003 Jonathon's income was $70 000 and Sarah, who worked on a casual basis due to parenting commitments, had an income of $20 000. Sarah decided to apply for a child support assessment and logged on to the Child Support Agency's website for an estimate. After entering their income levels and the children's details, Sarah discovered Jonathon would be required to pay her $15 730 annually (approximately $301 per week). Sarah then went ahead and made a formal application to the Agency.

Effect on your Family Tax Benefit

If you receive more than the base rate of the Family Tax Benefit you have to take reasonable action to get child support. This can be done in one of two ways. You can apply to the Child Support Agency for an assessment or you can come up with your own agreement and have it registered with the Agency. If the latter is chosen, Centrelink has to approve the agreement and it may not do so if the sum is less than the amount set by the formula.

Child maintenance trusts

Are you the parent paying rather than receiving child support? You might want to look into child maintenance trusts. Basically they offer a way for you to provide for your children without giving your ex control of the assets. One major advantage of child maintenance trusts is that income applied for maintenance is taxed at normal tax rates, as opposed to the staggeringly high children's tax levels.

It's not quite so simple, however. A child maintenance trust must meet certain requirements:

- property must be transferred into the trust;
- the property must vest in the children when the trust ends; and
- income generated must be on an arm's length basis.

Legal and financial advice should be sought.

Spousal maintenance

What about money for yourself? This issue is treated differently. Partners have an obligation to maintain each other and this duty can survive the end of the marriage. Spousal maintenance is not awarded in each case, however. Applications can be made at the Family Court, the Federal Magistrates Court, or the Local/Magistrates Court (the name of the latter varies between states). Courts will consider the particular needs of the applicant and the capacity of the other to pay.

More specifically, the court will consider both partners':

- age;
- health;
- standard of living;
- income, property and finances;
- ability to earn an income or retrain for future employment opportunities; and
- degree to which the marriage has affected earning capacity.

Legal advice should be sought. See the checklist on page 178 for the types of documents you should take to your lawyer. It's possible (and preferable) to come up with your own agreement regarding maintenance. A court must approve the agreement before registering it. De facto partners have limited rights to spousal maintenance in some states, including New South Wales.

Changing times

Alice was married for 30 years, spending all that time as a mother and home maker. She had never entered the workforce and since separating discovered she couldn't get a job. She applied for spousal maintenance and was awarded a reasonable sum.

However one of her daughters, Katie, found she was unable to receive spousal maintenance when she left her husband at about the same time. Katie had only been married for four years. Throughout that time she continued working, taking off only a few months when she had a baby. Although she wasn't entitled to spousal maintenance Katie was able to claim child support.

REMARRYING—WHAT ARE THE FINANCIAL IMPLICATIONS?

With a bit of luck things will turn out better the second time around. If you remarry or enter into a de facto relationship, be aware that there will be financial ramifications.

Child support

Generally the natural parent is still responsible for paying child support. There can be exceptions, however. If your new partner adopts your children, he or she takes over legal responsibility for care of the children. This includes the duty to provide for them financially. Conversely, if your ex partner takes on a legal duty to provide for other children—for instance by adopting or having other children—he or she might be able to have the amount of child support payable to you changed.

Spousal maintenance

Most likely any entitlements you might have to spousal maintenance from your former spouse will be lost.

Social security

Be sure to notify Centrelink if you remarry or enter into a de facto relationship. Most benefits are paid on the basis of both partners' income and assets. Your eligibility may have changed.

IF YOUR PARTNER DIES

This is right up there with the most stressful things that can ever happen. You may have come across the Social Readjustment Ratings Scale, devised by American doctors Holmes and Rahe. It ranks various life events according to the amount of adjustment needed to cope with them. Death of a spouse is ranked number one.

If your partner dies you will have to cope with many things, including financial strain, right at the time when you're least able to handle the pressure. There is help out there, however. You just need to know where to turn.

PAYING FOR THE FUNERAL

Unless you've been involved in arranging a funeral before you tend not to realise just how expensive they can be. The average funeral costs around $5000, but prices vary markedly depending on the choices you make. Prices of coffins/caskets vary by hundreds of dollars, as do the costs of headstones and other types of memorials. And if you are buying a burial plot in a major city, expect to pay far more than you would for the equivalent in a remote country town.

When a loved one dies there is a subtle but strong social pressure to spend more than you can afford. Try not to let other people push you further than you can go. You knew your partner best and it's up to you to decide what is appropriate.

Help with the costs

The deceased might have already made some provision for the funeral costs, for instance by taking out funeral insurance (a form of life insurance with a quick payout), purchasing funeral bonds or entering into a prepaid funeral plan. If not, you'll have to pay for it yourself.

You can seek reimbursement for the funeral costs from your partner's estate. Given this reduces the sum you inherit it doesn't sound like much help, but there is a plus here. Funeral costs are given a high priority when it comes to paying out the estate's debts. If there isn't enough money in the estate to meet all claims, the funeral expenses could well be paid ahead of other creditors' claims.

You might be entitled to receive some form of financial assistance from any of the following:

- Centrelink. Although an actual funeral benefit is not paid, you might be eligible for general financial assistance. If you receive an eligible pension, benefit or allowance you may be entitled to the Bereavement Payment. The Bereavement Allowance might help people who have not been receiving a Centrelink payment and do not have dependent children. The Widow Allowance is for women aged over 50 who have no recent workforce experience. The Parenting Payment provides help with the costs of raising children, paid to the primary carer. Income and assets tests apply. Payments are made in many varied circumstances so it is worth contacting Centrelink to see if you are eligible.
- Department of Veterans' Affairs (DVA). The DVA might pay a lump sum funeral benefit to help pay for an eligible veteran's funeral. (In 2003 the sum payable was up to $572.) Pensioner partners might also be entitled to a bereavement payment. The Office of Australian War Graves, which is part of the DVA, might meet the costs of official memorials for war veterans. Contact the Department for more details.
- Private health fund. Some offer a funeral benefit when a member dies. It's worth checking.
- Trade union. Some provide funeral benefits for members. Again, give them a call to see.

The funeral director might be willing to be paid by instalments. This is best discussed when you initially make the funeral arrangements, but still worth raising later if you find you are having difficulties.

YOUR FAMILY'S LIVING EXPENSES

When you are plunged into meeting major outlays such as funeral and possibly medical costs, it can be hard to meet daily living expenses. And it may be a long time before a deceased person's assets become available. This is particularly so if probate (court authorisation to deal with the will) or letters of administration (authority to deal with the estate where there is no will) are required.

So what can you do in the meantime? The following checklist can help keep your family afloat during those early dark days.

Checklist—Keeping afloat

For money to keep you and your children going, consider the following options:

- The survivor can usually still access joint bank accounts.
- Banks might release funds in low balance accounts that are in the deceased's sole name if you provide documents such as the will and death certificate. They might also release money for funeral costs if you produce the funeral director's invoice.
- Banks might agree to lend money using your interest in the estate as security. You will, however, end up paying fees and interest on the loan.
- You may be entitled to financial assistance with funeral costs (see page 185).
- Contact Centrelink for help with general living expenses (see page 185).
- Life insurance companies should be notified. They might pay out the policy without the need for probate or letters of administration if the sum due is under $50 000.
- Superannuation benefits may be available. Contact the superannuation trustee.

Keeping it together

Elaine's husband died after a brief but intense battle with cancer, leaving her to raise their three young children alone. Elaine was left with substantial medical costs and a $3900 funeral bill. She had access to their joint account but didn't have enough to pay for everything in one go. Fortunately her husband's health fund had a funeral benefit, which contributed $1000 to the cost of the funeral. His employer sponsored super was the greatest help, but took longer to be paid out than Elaine would have liked. She contacted Centrelink to see if she were eligible for any assistance, and was advised to put in an application for the Parenting Payment.

Elaine decided that, for the long-term benefit of her children and to help her deal with her grief, she would need to re-enter the workforce. Her mother agreed to help transport the children to and from school and mind them after school. Life would never be the same again but at least Elaine and her children could keep their heads above water.

Are you liable for your partner's debts if he or she dies?

You may be liable for your partner's debts if you were a joint debtor—in other words, if you incurred the debt with the deceased. A common example is taking out a home loan together. You may also be liable if you acted as guarantor—that is, if you guaranteed to pay the debt if your partner defaulted on the loan.

In other situations the money to pay your partner's debts will come out of their estate, not directly out of your pocket. This means, of course, there'll be less for you and your children to inherit. But if there isn't enough money in the estate to pay everything off, the estate might be declared insolvent. Processes similar to bankruptcy determine the distribution of assets to creditors, and not all creditors might be paid out.

COMPENSATION TO RELATIVES

Depending on the circumstances surrounding the death, you might be entitled to some form of compensation. Laws are complex and vary markedly between jurisdictions. Be sure to seek legal advice if death was the result of:

- a work injury—workers' compensation might be available;
- a motor vehicle accident—compulsory third party insurance might cover claims;

- a crime—criminal injuries or victim's compensation schemes might operate; or
- someone's wrongful act or negligence and your partner, if he or she had survived, may have had the right to sue for damages (for instance the death occurred on someone's property and the occupier was negligent).

FURTHER HELP

- Family Court of Australia—for information regarding divorce, property settlements and other family breakdown matters. Phone numbers can be found in the *White Pages* and see http://www.familycourt.gov.au.
- Child Support Agency—if you are separated. Call 131 272 and see their website at http://www.csa.gov.au.
- Centrelink and the Family Assistance Office. The number to call is 136 150 for information regarding family assistance and/or the Parenting Payment. For other types of benefits or to make an appointment call 131 021. Visit http://www.centrelink.gov.au and http://www.familyassist.gov.au.
- Department of Veterans' Affairs—for help with eligible veteran's funeral costs. Call 133 254 and see http://www.dva.gov.au.

Useful publications

Centrelink July 2003, 'Are you needing help after someone has died? A guide to prepare for and cope with bereavement', Centrelink.

Centrelink July 2003, 'Have you recently separated or divorced? A guide to your options and our services', Centrelink.

Family Court of Australia 2002, *The Family Court Book*, 3rd edn.

Star, L. 1998, *Making sense of the Family Court*, Choice Books, Sydney.

Tarakson, S. 2001, *What to Do When Someone Dies*, Choice Books, Sydney.

15

Beyond your lifetime

Death is something nobody wants to dwell on. The idea of our own mortality is unsettling, to say the least, and so we don't think about it. Deep down we all know we should make provision for what happens to our family. But not right now. We're too busy living life. And besides, there's plenty of time, right?

Well, maybe. And maybe not.

Once you have children you owe it to them to give some thought to these matters. You don't need to become morbidly obsessed—just dedicate a few days to planning, follow the proper procedures, then put it behind you.

PROTECTING YOUR FAMILY'S FINANCIAL WELLBEING

It's a natural instinct for parents to wish to provide for their children, even beyond their own lifetimes. Making a will is the obvious starting point. You can determine who gets what, set up trusts for children, and express your wishes on a crucial matter—who raises your kids if the worst happens. Life insurance is another thing to look at. You probably didn't need it when you were single, but things change when you have a family.

One thing many of us overlook is what happens if, rather than dying, we lose mental capacity. What would the effect be on your family if you were unable to deal with your assets and financial affairs? An enduring power of attorney can allow a trusted person to deal with these matters on your behalf.

This chapter examines all of these issues.

WILLS

Where there's no will

People often think that when they die their family can simply divide their assets as they see fit. Wrong. If you die without a will—which is known as dying intestate—the law decides who gets what. Property is distributed among your next of kin according to the intestacy formula. It's strict, it's rigid, and may not comply with your wishes. Even if you are happy with the formula, it's still quicker and cheaper in the long run if you have a will.

Intestacy formula

Categories of potential recipients exist. If anyone from a certain category is alive, all those on lower ranking groups are immediately excluded—meaning they get nothing. An exception exists where someone leaves behind a spouse and children. The children *might* be entitled to a share, depending on the value of the estate and state laws.

In New South Wales, for instance, children are only entitled to a share if the estate is over $150 000. The spouse takes the first $150 000, household chattels, and half of whatever's left over. The kids get the other half, to be divided among them in equal shares. The spouse can choose to keep the family home in full or part payment of her or his share, even if the value of the home exceeds $150 000.

Variations exist between states, but generally the order of categories is:

- spouse (in some states de facto and same sex partners have rights; things get complicated if there's both a legal spouse and a de facto or same sex partner);
- children (or, if a child is deceased, that child's children are eligible to receive his or her share);
- parents;
- brothers and sisters;
- grandparents; then

- aunts and uncles (in some states cousins can receive a share if the aunt/uncle is deceased).

If there's more than one person alive in a category they generally are entitled to equal shares. For example where there's no partner but two children, they are entitled to half each.

How the formula works

Elizabeth was a widow when she died intestate. She had two children, Henry and Jane. Henry, who was alive when his mother died, had one child. Jane had predeceased her mother but left two children. All three grandchildren were alive on Elizabeth's death. So who gets what?

As one of two children Henry is entitled to half of Elizabeth's estate. Under the intestacy formula his child receives nothing as Henry is alive. Jane would have been entitled to the other half but, being dead, her children effectively step into her shoes and are eligible to receive the share of the estate their mother would have been entitled to. Jane's children are entitled to one quarter of the estate each.

Possible injustices

Sometimes the intestacy formula can lead to serious injustices. Take the case of Mary. She was a young woman with two small children. The children's father had long since abandoned them, but she later met and married Simon. Like most young people, she gave little thought to dying. She was healthy and vital and put all of her energy into raising her family. Then she discovered her husband Simon was having an affair. She took the kids and left. Simon abandoned their rented home and moved in with his new girlfriend. Before Mary could apply for a divorce she was the tragic victim of a fatal hit and run accident.

Under the laws of her state the value of her estate was too low for her children to be eligible for a share. Simon was entitled to all of Mary's assets: her savings, investments and her car. Simon decided to use the money to help improve his girlfriend's house. Mary's two children received nothing. They moved in with her sister, but without the benefit of Mary's assets. Mary could have avoided this situation by writing a will and creating trusts for her children.

Trusts for under-age children

Children under eighteen can't inherit property outright, so a trust needs to be established for them. Property is invested on their behalf and the trustee must act in a prudent manner so as to maintain or improve the value of the asset over time.

You can create the trust in your will, in which case it is known as a testamentary trust. The trust only comes into operation on your death, so while you're alive you retain full ownership of the assets. You can use your will to appoint the trustee and provide him or her with certain powers to carry out your wishes. For example, many people use testamentary trusts to protect their estate from the claims of stepchildren and future spouses. You can also specify when the trust will end, as long as your child is eighteen or over by that date.

If you don't create a trust in your will and a beneficiary is under eighteen, a trust will need to be created anyway, but you won't be there to dictate the terms.

Children's non-wage earnings are taxed at very steep rates: see Chapter 13, 'Securing your children's financial future'. This is not the case, however, for income derived from a deceased estate, which is taxed at normal tax rates.

Anybody wishing to create a testamentary trust should seek legal advice.

A matter of trust

Janet recently inherited her parents' house and became the sole owner. She decided to leave it in her will to her three children, who were all under eighteen. With the help of a lawyer she set up a testamentary trust. She appointed her husband as trustee and stipulated that the trust should end when her youngest child turned 21. At that time the children would be entitled to inherit it outright in equal shares. She added a stipulation that if her husband should die before that time, her brother would become the trustee.

Trusts for children with disabilities

People who have children with intellectual or physical disabilities should also give some thought to setting up trusts. Rather than ending when the child reaches a certain age, these trusts might need to continue throughout the child's lifetime. Expert advice is crucial.

Testamentary guardians

This may well be the hardest decision you will ever need to make. If something were to happen to you and your partner, who would raise your children? It's a huge ask, so be sure to discuss it with the person you select. Naming them in your will as guardian does not legally oblige them to take on the task.

But what happens if you don't appoint someone and the worst happens? Your closest relatives are asked if they are willing and able to take on your children. Problems can arise if there's a dispute over who takes them. Mind you, that's not to say conflicts don't arise even where you do name a guardian. But at least then the court can take your wishes into account. The final yardstick, however, is what is in the children's best interests.

In the highly disturbing situation where there's no-one willing and able to take on your children, they may become wards of the state and may need to be placed in foster care. This is usually a last resort.

Duty to provide for your family

Family provision legislation requires testators (people drawing up wills) to make adequate provision for their dependants and close family members. If you don't, your will might be challenged.

Laws vary somewhat between states, but the following people might be able to challenge a will:

- spouse (in some states this can include a de facto or same sex partner);

- former spouse;
- children (this includes adopted and ex-nuptial children, and in some states it includes stepchildren);
- grandchildren who at some stage were dependent on the deceased (dependency needs to be proven); or
- others who at some stage were dependent on the deceased and who at some stage lived in the same household (again, dependency needs to be proven in this category).

You might, however, have a very strong reason for wanting to disinherit someone. If this is the case, seek legal advice. Generally courts will consider a testator's reasons for wanting to cut someone out of their will (often written in a separate sealed letter) but won't deprive someone of their share unless they think it is warranted.

Costs of making a will

So how do you get a will drawn up, and how much will it cost? You have several choices. You can:

- see a solicitor. Charges vary, but expect to pay around $100 for a simple will. More is charged for complex wills, for instance those containing trusts.
- go to a trustee company, private or public. Each state has a government run Public Trustee (known as the State Trustee in Victoria). Trustee companies usually prepare wills free of charge on the condition that you appoint them as executor or at least co-executor. They take a fee for administering your estate after your death. Fees are calculated on a percentage of the estate's value. Sliding scales are often used, so that as the value of the estate increases, the percentage charged falls. A maximum of about 4 to 5 per cent is fairly standard. If all you have in mind is a simple split of basic assets, this can prove to be a costly option.
- see a charity. Some draw up wills without charge if you name the charity as a beneficiary.

- do-it-yourself. Only attempt to write your own will if you have something simple in mind and you thoroughly research the matter first. Minor mistakes can lead to significant problems further down the track, which generally take a lot of time and money to resolve through the courts.

Checklist—planning your will

When planning your will you need to decide:

- who to appoint as executor (the person or body who is to administer your estate).
- who to appoint as testamentary guardian.
- whether you want to include funeral directions. It's wise to discuss your wishes with your family and not rely solely on your will as it may not be found until too late.
- the details of any trusts you may wish to establish, including whom to appoint as trustee.
- how you want to divide your property. Work out specific gifts if desired, but be sure to name someone who receives the residue (the rest of your assets).

Updating your will

Once you've made your will don't stash it away and forget it. Wills need to be updated if:

- you get married. Marriage can automatically revoke a will, unless the will was specifically written in contemplation of marriage. Even so, it's best to be on the safe side.
- you enter a same sex or de facto relationship.
- you divorce. The effect of divorce on a will varies between states. It could revoke the gift to your ex, revoke the whole will, or have no effect at all. Again, be on the safe side.
- you have or adopt a child.
- a beneficiary or executor dies.
- your assets change significantly.
- several years have passed since you last looked at your will.
- you retire.

LIFE INSURANCE

This is another of those unsettling things that you really need to consider once you have children.

Who needs it?

Young single people with no dependants may not yet need life insurance. Empty nesters reaching retirement age have a declining need. So those who should give it the most serious consideration are those in-between. In other words, people with young families and particularly those with large debts, such as an outstanding home loan.

Obviously the breadwinner in the family needs adequate life insurance to protect his or her family from the loss of income if he or she dies. If both partners earn an income they should both consider their need for insurance.

But what about non-working or low income spouses? They often believe they don't need life insurance as their family doesn't rely on their income. But there's a lot more to it than that. Chances are that the breadwinner will have to keep on working to support the children, rather than being able to stay home to look after them on a full-time basis. He or she may need to employ a nanny, and perhaps some help with the housekeeping. Without life insurance it might be hard to stretch finances far enough.

Are you doubling up?

Life insurance is often a component of employer-sponsored superannuation funds. If you take out a separate policy you might be doubling up. Check your super fund first to determine whether it includes a life insurance component, and if it does, whether it's adequate. Consider the size of the payout and the size of your debts and family's living expenses including education, extracurricular and lifestyle expenses.

Types of life insurance

Basically, there are two types:

- term insurance. This is taken out for a specified period of time. You are only covered while the policy is in operation. Premiums usually increase with age. It becomes harder to get insurance as you grow older and start to develop more health risks.
- whole of life insurance. As well as providing term life cover, whole of life policies carry an investment component. Your premiums (minus fees and expenses) are invested to increase the final value of your policy. Premiums are generally level throughout the life of the policy. Cancelling before maturity significantly reduces the payout under the policy. New sales of whole of life insurance policies are very low.

Knee deep in debt

Jason and Sandra have two small children, both too young for school. Sandra is a full-time mother but plans to look for a job when both children are at school. Jason is currently the sole breadwinner and has employer-sponsored super.

After years of saving they have just bought their first home. Their home loan is large enough to give them a serious case of the jitters. The bank suggested they consider life insurance, something they had overlooked up until now.

Jason investigated the life insurance aspect of his super and decided it was insufficient given his new level of debt. He decided to top up the level of cover. Sandra has no super at the moment. She took out a term life insurance policy that would pay a lump sum sufficient to cover the costs of a full-time nanny and housekeeper if necessary.

Related insurance products

Apart from straight-out standard life insurance, you may also want to consider:

- income protection insurance, to cover the possibility that you may become ill or have an accident that prevents you working for an extended time. Employees are covered by sick leave but usually only for a short period. Income protection insurance provides an ongoing income while you are unable to work.

- total or permanent disability insurance, to cover the possibility that you may suffer an injury or illness that prevents you from ever returning to work. But what sort of work? You might still be able to earn some sort of income, and so might not be covered. Make sure you are clear about the terms of the policy.
- trauma or crisis insurance, to cover the possibility that you may suffer from a life threatening or major debilitating condition specified in the policy. Common examples are heart attack or stroke. This insurance is usually paid as a lump sum.

These related forms of cover are often available as stand alone policies. They are also often packaged up and included as components of a broader life insurance policy.

Shopping for insurance

The amount of cover you require depends on your assets, your liabilities and your family responsibilities. Your insurance needs are by no means straightforward, and policies vary significantly in what they cover. Even definitions of basic terms such as 'income' and 'disability' vary between policies, and the consequences can be considerable. Professional advice should be sought when shopping for life insurance and related products. The services of a financial planner or insurance broker are worth considering.

LOSS OF CAPACITY

Something we often overlook is what would happen to our children if—rather than dying—we lose the mental capacity to manage our affairs. Normally this is an issue of old age but sometimes accidents can have tragic consequences. On our death our estate passes, either through a will or by the laws of intestacy, but what happens if you are still alive and unable to deal with your assets?

Someone may have to apply to a court or tribunal for authority to be appointed as your financial manager. This person could be a family member, a friend, professional or a government body, but you won't be in a position to have your say. The process takes time and adds to the high degree of stress your family would already be under.

Power of attorney

A power of attorney overcomes this problem. This legal document allows you (the donor or principal) to authorise someone (the attorney or agent) to act on your behalf. You can appoint a relative, friend, lawyer, accountant or trustee company. You can appoint more than one, giving them the ability to act 'jointly and/or severally', that is, together and/or independently.

The greatest consideration when making your choice is trust. The power conferred is great and the potential for misuse is undeniably there. Many people choose their partner or, if elderly, their adult child jointly with their partner. This is a matter only you can decide.

There are two types of powers of attorney:

- Ordinary powers of attorney can be limited in their grant of powers and time of operation. They are useful if you are travelling overseas, for instance, and want someone at home to have the ability to pay off your credit card bills and such. Or they can be unlimited, giving your attorney or agent wide ranging abilities. If you later lose mental capacity, an ordinary power of attorney stops working.
- Enduring powers of attorney continue to operate even if you lose mental capacity, providing a very effective safety net, particularly for the elderly.

Both types of instruments stop operating when the donor or principal dies, so remember they are not a substitute for a will which operates from death.

In most states enduring powers of attorney only confer the power to deal with property and financial matters. In some states (for example the Australian Capital Territory and Queensland) the instruments can also cover the ability to make medical and/or lifestyle decisions. In the jurisdictions where they don't, other documents can (such as medical powers of attorney and enduring powers of guardianship).

Making a power of attorney

A power of attorney can only be made by someone who has sufficient mental capacity to understand the nature and intention of the document, as well as the consequences of signing it. The instrument can be created to start at once or at a later date.

If you are considering creating a power of attorney see a solicitor or a trustee company (public or private). You can revoke the instrument at any time as long as you retain mental capacity.

FURTHER HELP

- For information regarding wills and powers of attorney, you can contact the Public Trustee in your state (known as the State Trustee in Victoria). See the *White Pages* for contact details. Many have informative websites.
- Financial planners can help with life insurance needs. The Financial Planning Association has details of members. Call 1800 626 393 and visit their website at http://www.fpa.asn.au.

Useful publications

Renton, N.E. 1999, *Wills and Estate Planning*, Wrightbooks, Melbourne.

Redfern Legal Centre 1999, *Rest Assured: A Legal Guide to Wills, Estates and Funerals*, Redfern Legal Centre Publishing, Sydney.

Tarakson, S. 2001, *What to Do When Someone Dies*, Choice Books, Sydney.

Conclusion

So there you go. Everything you need to know about the costs of raising a family, including how to trim those costs without detriment to your children.

Although this book is about money, it's also about something far more important. It's about being free to enjoy your children—and enjoy them without forever fretting about financial matters.

If you already have children, you will know there is nothing to compare with the joy they can bring. It's not the sort of thing that can be measured in dollars and cents.

My brother had a child several years before I did. The look of contented bliss on his face when he looked at his baby daughter was something I could not relate to. Once when I took my niece to an activity centre I watched some of the parents while the kids played. They nearly all had that same look on their faces. You can bet they weren't thinking about the entrance fee.

Since then I've been lucky enough to wear that look too. I now have two great kids, aged four and seven.

Yes, it costs money to raise a family. Yes, you need to make financial sacrifices. But sometimes we get so caught up in life's daily struggles that we lose sight of the bigger picture.

My aim in writing this book is to help put things back into focus to allow you to tackle those monetary issues head on, leaving you free to enjoy your children more and worry less.

Because that's how it should be.

Glossary

Administrator: A person appointed by a court to deal with a deceased person's estate, where there is no appointed executor or the executor is unable or unwilling to act.

Assets: Things you own that have a monetary value.

Award: Legally binding document setting out the minimum conditions of employment, made under federal or state laws.

Balanced fund: A managed fund that invests over a range of markets: cash, shares, fixed interest and/or property.

Beneficiary: A person entitled to inherit under a will or benefit from a trust.

Bonds: Investment where money is lent to companies or governments for a certain term.

Capital: Amount of money invested.

Capital gains tax (CGT): A tax on the profit made from buying and selling particular types of assets.

Cash management trusts: A managed fund investing primarily in highly liquid securities such as bank bills and Treasury notes.

Child maintenance trusts: For parents with child support obligations, child maintenance trusts may offer a way to provide for children. A properly constructed trust's earnings are taxed at normal marginal tax rates, not children's tax levels.

Collective agreements: Agreements made between an employer and a group of employees or a union acting on their behalf.

Compound interest: Where interest earned from an investment is re-invested, thereby earning further interest.

Creditor: Someone who is owed money.

Debtor: Someone who owes money.

Decree absolute: Final court order made in divorce proceedings.

Decree nisi: Provisional court order in divorce proceedings. The divorce is not final until the decree absolute.

Dividend: Payment of a portion of a company's profits to shareholders.

Estate: Everything a person owns or has a financial interest in.

Estate planning: Setting up a person's affairs to achieve the desired result.

Excess: The part of an insurance claim that a policyholder agrees to pay out.

Executor: A person named in a will who is appointed the task of dealing with the deceased's estate and carrying out the provisions of the will.

Franking: Attaching tax credits to dividends based on the tax that has already been paid by the company.

Gap: The difference between the cost of medical treatment and the amount reimbursed.

Gearing: Borrowing money to invest.

Goods and Services Tax (GST): A broad based tax on the sale or supply of most goods and services sold within Australia. Currently 10 per cent.

Imputation: The system where shares are franked, meaning that tax credits are attached to dividends based on the tax already paid by the company.

Income: Money earned from working or investing, including wages, interest, dividends, rent.

Income protection insurance: Type of insurance that provides cover if you are unable to work due to an injury or illness.

Income splitting: Allocating income to another person, usually someone on a lower marginal tax rate.

Insurance premium: Money paid in order to be covered by an insurance policy.

Interest: A sum paid by a person borrowing money to the lender, as a percentage of the amount borrowed.

Intestacy: Dying without leaving a valid will.

Investment: Laying out money to earn a return such as rent, interest, dividend, profit.

Job sharing: The splitting of a full-time position between two employees.

Joint tenancy: The ownership of an asset by more than one person so that when one person dies, the surviving co-owner automatically inherits their share.

Letters of administration: A court order granting authority for a person to act as administrator of a deceased person's estate where no will was left.

Liabilities: Things you are responsible for, such as the repayment of a loan.

Life insurance: Term life insurance provides cover if you die. Whole of life insurance bundles term insurance with an investment product.

Litigation: Court action.

Managed fund: An investment product that pools together the money contributed by a large group of investors, and then invests it in various markets. Offered by funds managers and insurance companies.

Mediation: A dispute resolution process involving face-to-face discussion in the presence of a neutral person who facilitates the discussion but cannot impose a solution.

Mortgage: A loan that is secured by property.

Negative gearing: Borrowing to invest, where the costs of the investment are greater than the money being earned.

Partnership: Two or more people who run a business together.

Power of attorney: A formal document where a person can authorise another to act on his or her behalf regarding financial matters.

Pre-nuptial agreement: Document made before marriage purporting to deal with property rights on separation and divorce. More correctly known as financial agreements. Financial agreements can also be made during a marriage or after separation.

Principal: The amount borrowed when a loan is taken out. Also the amount put into an investment.

Probate: A court order establishing the validity of a deceased person's will and granting the executor the ability to deal with the estate.

Prospectus: A document issued by a company seeking to solicit funds from the general public (for example, a share or bond issue), setting out the offer and all the information reasonably necessary to make the decision. For a managed fund, the equivalent document is called a product disclosure statement.

Real terms: When we look at the value of something in real terms, we are adjusting for inflation.

Reasonable benefit limit: The maximum amount of superannuation benefit you can take at concessionally taxed rates. Different limits exist for money withdrawn as a lump sum and for where at least half is taken in the form of a qualifying pension or annuity.

Salary sacrifice: Forgoing some salary to receive other benefits, such as a higher superannuation contribution from the employer.

Saving: Putting money aside to meet future needs.

Shares/stocks: Part ownership of a company.

Sole trader: A person who runs a business on their own.

Stockbroker: A person who buys and sells shares on behalf of investors.

Superannuation: A form of retirement investment that carries tax concessions. Generally, the money is locked away until retirement.

Superannuation Guarantee Charge: A duty on employers to contribute a percentage of qualifying employees' salary into a superannuation fund on the employees' behalf.

Tax deduction: An expense that reduces your assessable income before tax is calculated.

Tax offset: A concession that allows you to reduce your tax bill by the amount of the offset. Previously known as a rebate.

Telecommuting: Working from a home-based office and keeping in touch with the employer using telecommunications technology.

Tenancy in common: The ownership of an asset by more than one person so that when a co-owner dies, that person's share passes according to his or her will or by the laws of intestacy.

Term deposit: A deposit with a financial institution for a fixed period of time, for a fixed interest rate.

Testamentary guardian: A person named in a will who is to take on responsibility for children if the parents die.

Testator: A person who makes a will.

Trust: An arrangement where property is held on behalf of others, who are known as beneficiaries.

Trustee: A person or organisation that holds property on behalf of others.

Will: A legal document outlining how property is to be divided after a person's death. Various formal requirements must be met.

Workplace agreements: An individual agreement made between an employee and an employer, dealing with conditions of employment.

Index